Congressional Research Service

Cybersecurity: Selected Legal Issues

Edward C. Liu
Legislative Attorney

Gina Stevens
Legislative Attorney

Kathleen Ann Ruane
Legislative Attorney

Alissa M. Dolan
Legislative Attorney

Richard M. Thompson II
Legislative Attorney

April 20, 2012

Congressional Research Service

7-5700

www.crs.gov

R42409

CRS Report for Congress —————————————
Prepared for Members and Committees of Congress

Summary

The federal government's role in protecting U.S. citizens and critical infrastructure from cyber attacks has been the subject of recent congressional interest. Critical infrastructure commonly refers to those entities that are so vital that their incapacitation or destruction would have a debilitating impact on national security, economic security, or the public health and safety. This report discusses selected legal issues that frequently arise in the context of recent legislation to address vulnerabilities of critical infrastructure to cyber threats, efforts to protect government networks from cyber threats, and proposals to facilitate and encourage sharing of cyber threat information among private sector and government entities. This report also discusses the degree to which federal law may preempt state law.

It has been argued that, in order to ensure the continuity of critical infrastructure and the larger economy, a regulatory framework for selected critical infrastructure should be created to require a minimum level of security from cyber threats. On the other hand, others have argued that such regulatory schemes would not improve cybersecurity while increasing the costs to businesses, expose businesses to additional liability if they fail to meet the imposed cybersecurity standards, and increase the risk that proprietary or confidential business information may be inappropriately disclosed.

In order to protect federal information networks, the Department of Homeland Security (DHS), in conjunction with the National Security Agency (NSA), uses a network intrusion system that monitors all federal agency networks for potential attacks. Known as EINSTEIN, this system raises significant privacy implications—a concern acknowledged by DHS, interest groups, academia, and the general public. DHS has developed a set of procedures to address these concerns such as minimization of information collection, training and accountability requirements, and retention rules. Notwithstanding these steps, there are concerns that the program may implicate privacy interests protected under the Fourth Amendment.

Although many have argued that there is a need for federal and state governments, and owners and operators of the nation's critical infrastructures, to share information on cyber vulnerabilities and threats, obstacles to information sharing may exist in current laws protecting electronic communications or in antitrust law. Private entities that share information may also be concerned that sharing or receiving such information may lead to increased civil liability, or that shared information may contain proprietary or confidential business information that may be used by competitors or government regulators for unauthorized purposes.

Several bills in the 112th Congress would seek to improve the nation's cybersecurity, and may raise some or all of the legal issues mentioned above. For example, H.R. 3523 (Rogers (Mich.)-Ruppersberger) addresses information sharing between the intelligence community and the private sector. H.R. 3674 (Lungren) includes provisions regarding the protection of critical infrastructure, as well as information sharing. H.R. 4257 (Issa-Cummings) would require all federal agencies to continuously monitor their computer networks for malicious activity and would impose additional cybersecurity requirements on all federal agencies. S. 2102 (Feinstein) seeks to facilitate information sharing. S. 2105 (Lieberman) includes the information sharing provisions of S. 2102, as well as provisions relating to the protection of critical infrastructure and federal government networks. S. 2151 (McCain) and H.R. 4263 (Bono-Mack) also addresses information sharing among the private sector and between the private sector and the government. Many of these bills also include provisions specifically addressing the preemption of state laws.

Contents

Legal Issues Related to Protecting Critical Infrastructure 1
 Deference to Agency Decisions.. 2
  Availability of Judicial Review 3
  Questions of Fact... 4
  Interpretations of Law 4
 Liability Concerns 5
 Freedom of Information 6
 Ex Parte Communications 9
 Legislation in the 112th Congress 9
  H.R. 3674, PRECISE Act of 2011... 10
  S. 2105, Cybersecurity Act of 2012 10
Legal Issues Related to the Protection of Federal Networks 14
 EINSTEIN Overview 14
 EINSTEIN and the Fourth Amendment 15
  Monitoring Communications from Federal Employees... 18
  Monitoring Communications from Private Persons to Federal Employees 20
  Alternative to Traditional Warrant Requirement... 21
 Privacy and Civil Liberties Oversight 22
 Legislation in the 112th Congress 23
  S. 2105, Cybersecurity Act of 2012 23
  H.R. 3674, Promoting and Enhancing Cybersecurity and Information Sharing
   Effectiveness Act of 2012 (PRECISE Act) 24
  H.R. 4257, Federal Information Security Amendments Act of 2012 25
Legal Issues Related to Cybersecurity Threat Information Sharing 26
 Electronic Communications Privacy Act.. 27
 Antitrust Law.. 29
 Liability for Information Sharing 31
 Protection of Proprietary or Confidential Business Information...................................... 32
 Privacy and Civil Liberties... 32
 Legislation in the 112th Congress 33
  H.R. 3523, Cyber Intelligence Sharing and Protection Act of 2011, As Reported............ 33
  H.R. 3674, PRECISE Act.. 36
  S. 2102, Cybersecurity Information Sharing Act of 2012 37
  S. 2105, Cybersecurity Act of 2012 39
  S. 2151, SECURE IT Act 40
Preemption.. 42

Contacts

Author Contact Information.. 45

For many, the Internet has become inextricably intertwined with daily life. Many rely on it to perform their jobs, pay their bills, send messages to loved ones, track their medical care, and voice political opinions, among a host of other activities. Likewise, government and business use the Internet to maintain defense systems, protect power plants and water supplies, and keep other types of critical infrastructure running.[1] Consequently, the federal government's role in protecting U.S. citizens and critical infrastructure from cyber attacks has been the subject of recent congressional interest.[2]

This report discusses selected legal issues that frequently arise in the context of legislation to address vulnerabilities of private critical infrastructure to cyber threats, efforts to protect government networks from cyber threats, and proposals to facilitate and encourage sharing of cyber threat information amongst private sector and government entities. This report also provides an overview of the ways in which federal laws of these types may preempt or affect the applicability of state law.

Legal Issues Related to Protecting Critical Infrastructure

Although no federal statute currently imposes a generally applicable obligation on businesses in the private sector to take measures to protect themselves from cyber vulnerabilities, Congress has chosen to impose regulatory standards regarding the security, including the cybersecurity, of specific sectors or types of private entities.[3] For example,[4] chemical facilities are subject to chemical facility anti-terrorism standards (CFATS) promulgated by the Department of Homeland Security (DHS), which include provisions requiring chemical facilities to take measures to protect against cyber threats.[5] Electrical utilities are required to comply with reliability standards, including standards to protect against cyber incidents, set by the North American Electrical Reliability Corporation (NERC).[6] Similarly, the Maritime Transportation Security Act (MTSA) gives the Coast Guard the authority to regulate the security of maritime facilities and vessels, including requiring security plans that contain provisions for the security of communications systems used in those facilities.[7]

---

[1] Critical infrastructure commonly refers to those entities that are so vital that their incapacitation or destruction would have a debilitating impact on national security, economic security, or the public health and safety. 42 U.S.C. §5195c(e). For more information, *see* CRS Report RL30153, *Critical Infrastructures: Background, Policy, and Implementation*, by John D. Moteff.

[2] *See, e.g.*, Siobhan Gorman, *Cybersecurity Bills Duel Over Rules for Firms*, WALL ST. J., March 9, 2012, at A6.

[3] *See also* GOVERNMENT ACCOUNTABILITY OFFICE, Information Technology: Federal Laws, Regulations, and Mandatory Standards for Securing Private Sector Information Technology Systems and Data in Critical Infrastructure Sectors, GAO-08-1075R, September 16, 2008, *available at* http://www.gao.gov/assets/100/95747.pdf.

[4] The existing regulatory frameworks discussed here do not constitute an exhaustive list of all regulations applicable to critical infrastructure, but are only intended to provide some context for the following discussions.

[5] P.L. 109-295, §550 (codified at 6 U.S.C. §121 note). For a more detailed discussion of CFATS, *see* CRS Report R41642, *Chemical Facility Security: Issues and Options for the 112th Congress*, by Dana A. Shea.

[6] For a more detailed discussion of cybersecurity and electrical utilities, see CRS Report R41886, *The Smart Grid and Cybersecurity—Regulatory Policy and Issues*, by Richard J. Campbell.

[7] 46 U.S.C. §§70102-70103.

Proposals that focus on the increased cybersecurity of certain sectors of the economy are frequently justified on the grounds that those private entities, including energy, transportation, or communication providers, comprise the nation's critical infrastructure. If the incapacity or destruction of such systems or assets would have a debilitating impact on national security, economic security, or public health and safety, it would be in the national interest to ensure that such critical infrastructure was adequately protected. Consequently, it has been argued that a regulatory framework governing selected critical infrastructure entities is needed to ensure that these private entities take measures adequate to maintain a minimum level of security from cyber threats, in order to protect the rest of the economy.[8]

On the other hand, others have argued that such regulatory schemes would not improve cybersecurity and would also increase the costs of doing business for these sectors of the economy.[9] There are also concerns that businesses would face additional exposure to civil liability from private suits if they failed to meet the imposed standards. As many of these regulatory schemes provide regulatory agencies with access to information held by the regulated entities, concerns have also been raised about the inappropriate disclosure of proprietary or confidential business information.

The concerns raised by these issues have shaped the existing legal schemes regulating the security of specific categories of critical infrastructure, and have also informed recent legislative proposals to address widely reported weaknesses in the security of critical infrastructure from cyber threats. A brief overview of each of these issues is provided in the next sections of this report. The report will then examine how recent cybersecurity legislation would specifically address some or all of these issues.

Deference to Agency Decisions

Several of the bills that would establish a regulatory scheme for the cybersecurity of critical infrastructure provide the agencies charged with administering the program with the discretion to identify those private entities that would fall within the scope of a particular bill and that will, therefore, be subject to the requirements that would be imposed under the bill. Being subject to the regulations may have significant cost, liability, or other implications for the private entity that has been designated as covered critical infrastructure; such entities may seek to challenge their designation as covered critical infrastructure through redress mechanisms created in the statute or through judicial review of agency action under the Administrative Procedure Act (APA).[10] Entities may also seek judicial review of agency actions in the context of enforcement actions taken against them under the various regulatory schemes.

---

[8] For a more detailed discussion of critical infrastructure policy arguments, see CRS Report RL30153, *Critical Infrastructures: Background, Policy, and Implementation*, by John D. Moteff.

[9] *E.g., Securing America's Future: The Cybersecurity Act of 2012 Before the S. Comm. on Homeland Security and Governmental Affairs*, 112th Cong. (statement of former DHS Secretary Tom Ridge on behalf of U.S. Chamber of Commerce) ("New compliance mandates would drive up costs and misallocate business resources without necessarily increasing security.")

[10] 5 U.S.C. §701 *et seq., see e.g.*, Nat'l Propane Gas Ass'n v. DHS, 534 F. Supp. 2d 16 (D.D.C. 2008) (denying temporary restraining order in action brought under APA claim for review of agency's designation of propane as chemical of interest for purposes of CFATS).

Depending upon the legislative language delegating regulatory authority to the agency, a court will evaluate an agency's decision under varying standards of review. In the context of regulating the security of critical infrastructure, a more deferential standard of review of agency determinations typically means that regulated private entities would have less recourse in the event that they wanted to challenge an agency's determination. On the other hand, a less deferential standard of review may extend the time to implement particular security standards if the agency encounters delays caused by litigation. Examples of the different types of judicial review that may be involved are discussed below.

Availability of Judicial Review[11]

As a general matter, there is a "'strong presumption that Congress intends judicial review' of administrative action."[12] This presumption is embodied in the Administrative Procedure Act (APA), which provides that "final agency action for which there is no other adequate remedy in a court [is] subject to judicial review."[13] The APA provides two exceptions to the presumption of availability of judicial review of agency action: (1) "to the extent that ... statutes preclude judicial review" and (2) "where agency action is committed to agency discretion by law."[14] However, judicial review of an unreviewable determination may occur if there is a constitutional issue.[15]

Under the APA, judicial review of agency actions may be unavailable if such review is specifically precluded by statute.[16] This exemption requires the existence of an explicit statutory provision prohibiting judicial review of agency action. Additionally, even where judicial review has not been explicitly barred, the APA precludes judicial review where the decision has been committed to agency discretion by law.[17] This second exemption has been interpreted by the Supreme Court to be a very narrow exception, and applies only in situations where the statute provides no law for a reviewing court to apply.[18] For example, in *Webster v. Doe*,[19] the Supreme Court held that firing decisions made by the Director of Central Intelligence were unreviewable because the National Security Act provided that the Director "may, in his discretion, terminate the employment of any officer or employee of the [Central Intelligence Agency] whenever he shall

---

[11] For more information on judicial review of agency actions, see CRS Report R41546, *A Brief Overview of Rulemaking and Judicial Review*, by Vanessa K. Burrows and Todd Garvey.

[12] Gutierrez De Martinez v. Lamagno, 515 U.S. 417, 424 (1995) (quoting Bowen v. Michigan Academy of Family Physicians, 476 U.S. 667, 670 (1986)); *see also* McNary v. Haitian Refugee Center, Inc., 498 U.S. 479, 496 (1991); Abbott Laboratories v. Gardner, 387 U.S. 136 (1967); Citizens to Protect Overton Park v. Volpe, 401 U.S. 402 (1971); 28 U.S.C. §1331; *but see* Block v. Community Nutrition Institute, 467 U.S. 340, 349 (1984) (noting that "[t]he presumption favoring judicial review of administrative action ... may be overcome by specific language or specific legislative history that is a reliable indicator of congressional intent"). "The congressional intent necessary to overcome the presumption may also be inferred from contemporaneous judicial construction barring review and the congressional acquiescence in it ... or from the collective import of legislative and judicial history behind a particular statute," or from "inferences of intent drawn from the statutory scheme as a whole." *Id.*

[13] 5 U.S.C. §§702, 704.

[14] 5 U.S.C. §701.

[15] *See* Webster v. Doe, 486 U.S. 592 (1988); Oestereich v. Selective Service System, 393 U.S. 233 (1968).

[16] 5 U.S.C. §701(a)(1).

[17] 5 U.S.C. §701(a)(2).

[18] Citizens of Overton Park v. Volpe, 401 U.S. 402 (1971).

[19] Webster v. Doe, 486 U.S. 592 (1988).

deem such termination necessary or advisable in the interests of the United States."[20] The Court held that such a statute "exuded deference" and noted:

> Short of permitting cross-examination of the Director concerning his views of the Nation's security and whether the discharged employee was inimical to those interests, we see no basis on which a reviewing court could properly assess an Agency termination decision.[21]

Since the statute contained no standards a court could apply to evaluate the Director's decision, the Court determined that these decisions had been committed to agency discretion by law, and were consequently unreviewable.

Questions of Fact

Where a statute does provide judicially administrable standards, agency determinations of factual questions are typically reviewed under the "substantial evidence" or "abuse of discretion standards."[22] In the administrative context, substantial evidence review and abuse of discretion review occur in factually distinct circumstances. Substantial evidence is required when an agency engages in either formal rulemaking or an adjudicatory hearing.[23] In contrast, abuse of discretion applies in cases of informal rulemaking and decisions.[24]

Some courts appear to consider substantial evidence a more demanding standard than abuse of discretion, but the consistent theme of both standards is that the court is not free to substitute its judgment in place of the agency's.[25] In terms of analysis, the substantial evidence and abuse of discretion standards are both less stringent than *de novo* review, which would allow a court to look at the evidence anew and come to its own conclusions. Nevertheless, the Supreme Court has described these standards as requiring "more than a mere scintilla" of support and comparable to the standard a trial judge must meet to sustain a jury's verdict.[26] In the federal courts, a jury verdict will not be disturbed if "reasonable and fair-minded persons in exercise of impartial judgment" might have come to the same conclusion as the jury.[27]

Interpretations of Law

Agencies may also exercise discretion in interpreting the terms used in a statute. In the context of the proposals to regulate the cybersecurity of critical infrastructure, which are discussed in more detail below, there are a number of provisions that may require the Secretary of Homeland

---

[20] 50 U.S.C. §403-4a(e)(1).

[21] *Webster*, 486 U.S. at 600.

[22] 5 U.S.C. §706(2).

[23] *Id.* at §706(2)(E).

[24] *Id.* at §706(2)(A).

[25] *See, e.g.*, Frontier Fishing Corp. v. Evans, 429 F. Supp. 2d 316, n.7 (citing Indus. Union Dep't v. API, 448 U.S. 607, 705 (1980) (Marshall, J., dissenting) (asserting that substantial evidence is more stringent, but is ultimately a deferential standard)).

[26] Consolidated Edison Co. v. NLRB, 305 U.S. 197, 229 (1938); NLRB v. Columbian Enameling & Stamping Co., 306 U.S. 292, 300 (1939)

[27] *E.g.*, Kosmynka v. Polaris Industries, Inc., 462 F.3d 74, 79-82 (2d Cir. 2006) (upholding jury's finding that a manufacturer was negligent for failing to warn that its all-terrain vehicle might upend itself despite uncontested evidence that the manufacturer had received no reports of such incidents).

Security (the Secretary) to use her discretion to interpret the language of the bills. For example, the various definitions for covered critical infrastructure used by the bills may require a finding that the disruption of a function, system, or asset would lead to harms that were "significant," "extraordinary," or "prolonged." These terms may be susceptible to more than one specific construction, and the different interpretations may have material consequences for those subject to the regulatory scheme. A narrow definition may mean that fewer entities would be subject to regulation, while a broader definition may encompass a more expansive cross-section of businesses.

The validity of an agency's construction of a statute would likely be evaluated using the two-prong test described by the Supreme Court in *Chevron v. Natural Resources Defense Council*.[28] First, if the text and legislative history of the statute demonstrate that Congress has spoken directly on the issue, then that statutory language or history must control. However, under the second prong, if the statute is ambiguous because "Congress has not directly addressed the precise question at issue," the agency's interpretation will stand so long as it is a reasonable one.[29]

Therefore, under *Chevron*, whether a particular statutory provision is ambiguous or not can change the degree of deference afforded an agency. Where no ambiguity exists, the reviewing court's focus is on the intent of Congress, and it may interpret the law *de novo* without any deference toward the agency's interpretation. On the other hand, if the statute is ambiguous, either because the language used is susceptible to more than one meaning or because the law contains internal inconsistencies, the reviewing court is not permitted to supplant its own interpretive preferences for that of the agency, unless the agency's interpretation is unreasonable. Under this deferential standard of review, the discretion available to an agency is inversely proportional to the degree of specificity provided in a particular statute. In the context of the bills discussed by this report, the less specific a particular bill is regarding the Secretary's regulatory authority, the more flexibility would be available to her to exercise during implementation.

Liability Concerns

The creation of a regulatory scheme applicable to critical infrastructure may raise issues regarding the effects that the new regulatory scheme would have on the potential civil or criminal liability of the covered entities. Regulators may be given the authority to impose civil or criminal penalties for noncompliance, or may seek to promote compliance by offering financial incentives.[30]

In addition to the forms of liability imposed by regulatory authorities, questions may arise regarding the potential ways in which the regulatory scheme may expose covered entities to additional private civil liability. In this context, a federal regulatory scheme could be viewed as creating a standard of care that might be used to establish tort liability under state law. Entities

---

[28] Chevron v. Nat'l Resources Def. Council, 467 U.S. 837, 842-45 (1984).

[29] *Id.*

[30] A second issue with respect to enforcement is whether penalties would be limited to fines and other monetary penalties or whether injunctive relief may also be sought to compel compliance or to stop a noncompliant facility from operating. For example, violations of CFATS can be punished by civil monetary penalties or an injunction to cease operations. 6 C.F.R. §27.300. Similarly, under MTSA, covered vessels and facilities without an approved security plan may be prohibited from operating. 46 U.S.C. §70103(c)(5). Questions may also arise regarding the types of investigative authorities that would be provided to the agency tasked with administering the regulatory scheme.

that fall below that standard of care face the possibility of liability in the event of a security breach, separate and apart from any penalties that might be imposed by government regulators. The most likely form that such a civil action would take is in a tort suit alleging that the private entity had acted negligently; that is, the entity had failed to exercise reasonable care in the face of a foreseeable risk. Under current state law, entities found negligent may be liable for harm that results from their negligence.[31]

The existence of a federal regulatory scheme that imposes compliance standards may affect suits alleging negligence in two ways. First, the entities that are subject to the compliance standards may be found negligent *per se* if they fail to satisfy those standards.[32] Negligence *per se* is a theory of negligence in which the fact that an entity's conduct has violated some applicable statute is *prima facie* evidence that the entity has acted negligently.[33] Unless the defendant could rebut that presumption, the defendant would likely be found to be *per se* negligent, and consequently liable for any harm that results from that negligence.[34] In the context of cyber threats to critical infrastructure, this might mean that a regulated entity that fails to adequately secure its information infrastructure as required under a federal regulatory scheme would be liable for a cyber incident that causes harm to customers or other third parties.

Second, entities that are not subject to regulation under a federal scheme may not be subject to negligence *per se*. However, the performance standards or other requirements imposed under that scheme may still affect their liability for negligence if such requirements establish an applicable standard of care that the nonregulated entity would be judged against in a private civil suit.[35]

Freedom of Information[36]

Access to the confidential business information of owners and operators of the nation's critical infrastructure and of private sector entities continues to be an important component of efforts to protect against cybersecurity threats. However, some critical infrastructure owners and operators and private sector entities may be hesitant to share cybersecurity-related information with the government because of the possible disclosure of this information to the public under the Freedom of Information Act (FOIA)[37] and state open records laws.[38] In addition, concerns also

---

[31] Reese v. Philadelphia & R. R. Co., 239 U.S. 463, 465 (1915) ("The rule is well settled that a railroad company is not to be held as guaranteeing or warranting absolute safety to its employees under all circumstances, but is bound to exercise the care which the exigency reasonably demands in furnishing proper roadbed, tracks, and other structures. A failure to exercise such care constitutes negligence.").

[32] *See* RESTATEMENT (SECOND) OF TORTS §285 ("The standard of conduct of a reasonable man may be ... adopted by the court from a legislative enactment or an administrative regulation which does not so provide ...").

[33] *See, e.g.*, Makas v. Hillhaven, Inc., 589 F. Supp. 736, 741 (M.D.N.C. 1984) ("Negligence *per se* in effect is a presumption that one who has violated a safety statute has violated its legal duty to exercise due care.").

[34] *See, e.g.*, Resser v. Boise-Cascade Corp., 587 P.2d 80, 84 (Or. 1978) (violation of state law establishing speed limits at railroad crossing raises a rebuttable presumption of negligence).

[35] *See, e.g.*, Burmaster v. Gravity Drainage Dist. No. 2, 448 So. 2d 162, 164 (La. Ct. App. 1984) (Occupational Safety and Health Act regulations and standards published by industry groups warrant consideration as evidence of standard of care, even if they are not controlling).

[36] *See* CRS Report R41406, *The Freedom of Information Act and Nondisclosure Provisions in Other Federal Laws* , by Gina Stevens and CRS Report RL33670, *Protection of Security-Related Information*, by Gina Stevens and Todd B. Tatelman.

[37] 5 U.S.C. §552.

[38] National Freedom of Information Coalition, State Freedom of Information Laws (2012), at http://www.nfoic.org/ (continued...)

---

exist that sharing of cybersecurity information may facilitate access to proprietary and confidential business information by competitors. Furthermore, some have expressed concerns that the government may use information obtained for cybersecurity purposes for non-cybersecurity purposes, such as regulatory actions. Concerns also exist that reliance on FOIA's exemptions to shield shared cybersecurity threat information is misplaced because court interpretations of the scope of FOIA's exemptions can change.[39] Proponents of open records and government transparency argue that new exemptions from FOIA jeopardize the public's ability to obtain information about government and industry practices, cast a shroud of secrecy over government's functions, and are unnecessary because FOIA's exemptions adequately protect private information from disclosure.[40] Some observers believe that it is not certain that some cybersecurity threat information, such as routing information or website access logs, would fit within FOIA's exemptions.

The Freedom of Information Act of 1974 (FOIA) regulates the disclosure of federal agency records.[41] FOIA requires that certain types of records be published in the *Federal Register*;[42] that certain types of records be made available for public inspection and copying;[43] and that all other records be subject to request in writing. All records not available via publication or inspection, not exempt from disclosure, or excluded from coverage are subject to disclosure.[44] FOIA has nine exemptions from disclosure which permit, rather than require, the withholding of the requested information.[45]

Subsection (b)(3) of FOIA, commonly referred to as exemption 3, permits agencies to withhold information under FOIA that is specifically prohibited from disclosure by other federal statutes.[46] For a nondisclosure provision in a separate federal statute to qualify for exemption 3 status, the nondisclosure provision must meet the following criteria: either the statute must require that matters be withheld from the public in such a manner as to leave no discretion on the issue; or the statute must establish particular criteria for withholding or refer to particular types of matters to be withheld; and it must specifically cite FOIA exemption 3.[47] If the statute meets the criteria of

---

(...continued)

state-freedom-of-information-laws.

[39] As an example, in Milner v. Dept. of the Navy, 131 S. Ct. 1259 (2011), the Supreme Court limited the scope of FOIA Exemption 2 (the Court held that "Exemption 2, consistent with the plain meaning of the term "personnel rules and practices," encompasses only records relating to issues of employee relations and human resources."). *Id.* at 1271. *See* U.S. Dep't of Justice, Exemption 2 After the Supreme Court's Ruling in *Milner v. Department of the Navy*, at http://www.justice.gov/oip/foiapost/2011foiapost15 html.

[40] Testimony of David Sobel, Electronic Privacy Information Clearinghouse before the U.S. Congress, House Committee on Energy and Commerce, Subcommittee on Oversight and Investigations, *Creating The Department of Homeland Security: Consideration of the Administration's Proposal*, 107th Cong., 2nd sess., June 25 and July 9, 2002, Serial No. 107-113 (Washington: GPO, 2002), p. 258.

[41] 5 U.S.C. §552.

[42] 5 U.S.C.§552(a)(1).

[43] 5 U.S.C. §552(a)(2).

[44] Excluded from the act's coverage are special categories of law enforcement records related to criminal law investigations or proceedings, informant records, and records maintained by the FBI pertaining to foreign intelligence, counterintelligence or international terrorism. 5 U.S.C. §552(c)(1), (c)(2), (c)(3).

[45] *See* Dep't of the Air Force v. Rose, 425 U.S. 352, 361 (1976) (holding that "limited exemptions do not obscure the basic policy that disclosure, not secrecy, is the dominant objective of the Act").

[46] 5 U.S.C. §552(b)(3).

[47] 5 U.S.C. §552(b)(3).

---

exemption 3 and the information to be withheld falls within the scope and coverage of FOIA, the information is exempt from disclosure under exemption 3.[48] Statutes that meet these criteria are referred to as "FOIA exemption 3 statutes."[49]

To encourage private and public sector entities and persons to voluntarily share their critical infrastructure information with the Department of Homeland Security (DHS), the Critical Infrastructure Information Act of 2002 (CIIA) includes several measures to ensure against disclosure of protected critical infrastructure information by DHS. According to the Department of Justice, the agency responsible for administering FOIA, the CIIA will operate as an exemption 3 statute under FOIA for critical infrastructure information that is obtained by the Department of Homeland Security.[50] Relevant to this discussion, the CIIA provides protections against the disclosure of information that is voluntarily submitted by a critical infrastructure entity to DHS. If the information submitted satisfies the requirements of the CIIA, the information is designated as critical infrastructure information (CII), and for purposes of FOIA, the CIIA expressly prohibits the disclosure of critical infrastructure information. Critical infrastructure information "means information not customarily in the public domain and related to the security of critical infrastructure or protected systems...."[51] Therefore, the classification of information as CII would protect that information from disclosure under FOIA, state and local disclosure laws, and use in civil litigation. In addition, protected critical infrastructure information cannot be used for regulatory purposes.[52] Federal, state, and local government officials and contractors approved by DHS can access the information for critical infrastructure protection or criminal law enforcement purposes.

With respect to concerns about litigation, CIIA limits the use of CII in civil litigation and provides that sharing CII with the agency does not count as the "waiver of any applicable privilege or protection provided under law," such as trade secret protection or the attorney-client privilege.[53] CIIA authorizes the use or disclosure of such information by officers and employees in furtherance of the investigation or the prosecution of a criminal act, or for disclosure to Congress or the Government Accountability Office.

Another Exemption 3 statute under FOIA for critical infrastructure information was recently enacted in the National Defense Authorization Act for Fiscal Year 2012. Section 1091 authorizes the Secretary of Department of Defense (DOD), or his designee, to exempt DOD critical

---

[48] U.S. Department of Justice, Statutes Found to Qualify under Exemption 3 of the FOIA, (August 2011), *available at* http://www.justice.gov/oip/exemption3.pdf.

[49] Examples of FOIA exemption 3 statutes are the Aviation and Transportation Security Act of 2001 (ATSA) which designates 16 categories of sensitive security information and includes information submitted pursuant to a requirement and information voluntarily submitted, P.L. 107-71, codified at 49 U.S.C. §40119; the Critical Infrastructure Information Act of 2002 (CIIA) which provides confidentiality protections for critical infrastructure information voluntarily submitted to DHS, P.L. 107-296, codified at 6 U.S.C. §133 *et seq.*; the Maritime Transportation Security Act of 2002 (MTSA) which requires covered entities to submit information to the federal government, P.L. 107-295; and the Safe Drinking Water Act (SDWA) , as amended, which requires community water systems to perform vulnerability analyses of their facilities and includes protections for vulnerability assessments. P.L. 107-188, 42 U.S.C. §300i-2.

[50] Department of Justice, "Homeland Security Law Contains New Exemption 3 Statute," FOIA Post (2003).

[51] 6 C.F.R. §29.2(b).

[52] *See* U.S. Dept. of Homeland Security, Protected Critical Infrastructure Information (PCII) Program, at http://www.dhs.gov/files/programs/editorial_0404.shtm; PCII Program and Procedures Guidance Manual (April 2009) at http://www.dhs.gov/xlibrary/assets/pcii_program_procedures_manual.pdf.

[53] *See* Fed. R. Evid. 501.

---

infrastructure security information from disclosure pursuant to section 552(b)(3) of title 5 [FOIA Exemption 3] upon a written determination that the information is DOD critical infrastructure security information, and the public interest consideration in the disclosure of such information does not outweigh preventing the disclosure of such information.[54] Department of Defense critical infrastructure security information means sensitive but unclassified information that, if disclosed, would reveal vulnerabilities of DOD critical infrastructure that could result in the disruption, degradation, or destruction of Department of Defense (DOD) operations, property, or facilities.

Ex Parte Communications

Providing information to a regulatory agency may also be subject to further disclosure if the communication would implicate agency rules or judicial doctrine regarding ex parte communications. Under the APA, formal agency adjudications are to be decided solely on the basis of record evidence. The APA provides that "[t]he transcript of testimony and exhibits, together with all papers and requests filed in the proceeding, constitutes the exclusive record for decision."[55] The reason for this "exclusiveness of record" principle is to provide fairness to the parties in order to ensure meaningful participation. Challenges to the "exclusiveness of record" occur when there are ex parte contacts—communications from an interested party to a decision-making official that take place outside the hearing and off the record.[56] The APA prohibits any "interested person outside the agency" from making, or knowingly causing, "any ex parte communication relevant to the merits of the proceeding" to any decision making official.[57] Similar restraints are imposed on the agency decision makers.[58] Additionally, ex parte communications received in violation of these rules are generally required to be disclosed to all other interested parties and made part of the public record for the proceeding.[59] The CIIA provides that CII will not be subject to agency rules or judicial doctrine regarding ex parte communications. However, if an entity is involved in a proceeding where ex parte communications are prohibited, there may be concerns that providing cybersecurity information that would not qualify as CII might implicate the rules against ex parte communications, and could be subject to disclosure on the public record or to other interested parties.

Legislation in the 112th Congress

This section provides a brief description of proposed cybersecurity legislation in the 112th Congress that includes regulatory provisions regarding the security of critical infrastructure with particular emphasis placed on the provisions that implicate the legal issues discussed above.

---

[54] P.L. 112-8, §1091, 125 Stat. 1604.

[55] 5 U.S.C. §556(e).

[56] *Id.*

[57] 5 U.S.C. §557(d)(1). For example, under CFATS, during an adjudication ex-parte communications between the department and the chemical facility is not permitted. 6 C.F.R. §27.320.

[58] 5 U.S.C. §557(d)(1)(E).

[59] 5 U.S.C. §557(d)(1)(C).

H.R. 3674, PRECISE Act of 2011

H.R. 3674, the Promoting and Enhancing Cybersecurity and Information Sharing Effectiveness Act of 2011 (PRECISE Act), was introduced on December 15, 2011, by Representative Lungren. On February 1, 2012, the Subcommittee on Cybersecurity, Infrastructure Protection, and Security Technologies of the House Homeland Security Committee held a mark up of the bill, and it was forwarded to the full committee by voice vote. On April 18, 2012, full committee consideration and mark up were held on a substitute bill that changed the critical infrastructure provisions. The measure was reported favorably to the full House (as amended) 16-13.

As introduced, Section 2 of the PRECISE Act would have authorized the Secretary of Homeland Security to identify and evaluate cybersecurity risks to critical infrastructure and to review and develop a collection of existing internationally recognized consensus-developed risk-based performance standards.[60] It would have given the Secretary the authority to designate particular facilities or functions of critical infrastructure companies as covered critical infrastructure.[61] Such entities would have been subject to more stringent regulation than noncovered critical infrastructure. Additionally, the PRECISE Act would have explicitly provided for judicial review of the designation of facilities or functions as covered critical infrastructure.[62]

On April 18, the full committee held a mark up and reported out a substitute bill. This version removed the proposed Section 227, which would have provided the Secretary its authority to designate particular facilities as critical infrastructure and develop the standards these entities would have been required to implement. Under the approved PRECISE Act, DHS may "solely upon the request of critical infrastructure owners and operators, assist such critical infrastructure owners and operators in protecting their critical infrastructure information systems."

S. 2105, Cybersecurity Act of 2012

S. 2105, the Cybersecurity Act of 2012, was introduced on February 14, 2012, by Senator Lieberman. Title I of the bill would create a regulatory scheme for the protection of selected systems and assets of critical infrastructure from cybersecurity threats. Specifically, the bill would authorize the Secretary of Homeland Security to identify cybersecurity risks to critical infrastructure,[63] designate certain assets or systems as "covered critical infrastructure,"[64] and identify performance standards that covered critical infrastructure would have to meet in order to guard against the identified cybersecurity risks.[65] If the Secretary determines that an existing regulatory scheme would adequately protect covered critical infrastructure from cyber threats, then no new performance standards would be imposed with respect to that covered critical infrastructure.[66]

---

[60] H.R. 3674, §2 (new §227 of the Homeland Security Act of 2002 (HSA)).

[61] *Id.* (new HSA §227(f)).

[62] *Id.* (new HSA §227(g)).

[63] S. 2105, §102.

[64] S. 2105, §103.

[65] S. 2105, §104.

[66] S. 2105, §104(d).

The potential applicability of this new regulatory regime to an entity would depend upon whether its systems or assets had been designated by the Secretary as covered critical infrastructure.[67] The bill would define covered critical infrastructure as systems or assets that, if damaged or accessed without authorization, could reasonably lead to the interruption of life sustaining services sufficient to cause a mass casualty event with an extraordinary number of fatalities or mass evacuations with a prolonged absence, catastrophic economic damage to the United States, or severe degradation of national security.[68] Catastrophic economic damage is defined to include the failure or substantial disruption of a U.S. financial market, transportation system, or other systemic, long-term damage to the U.S. economy.[69] Commercial information technology products[70] are statutorily precluded from being designated as covered critical infrastructure, as are systems or assets based solely on activities that are protected by First Amendment rights.[71]

Because of a perceived increased regulatory burden that might accompany a designation of a system or asset as covered critical infrastructure, some entities may wish to dispute such a designation. The Cybersecurity Act of 2012 would explicitly provide for judicial review of decisions to designate systems or assets as covered critical infrastructure.[72] Such review would likely involve both questions of fact as well as interpretations of the bill's language. Examples of factual questions that might be raised include whether the disruption of an asset could lead to a mass casualty event or degradation of national security. The Cybersecurity Act of 2012 does not specify a particular standard of review that courts should use when reviewing these questions. But, under the APA, a court is likely to apply a "substantial evidence" or "abuse of discretion" standard to these types of factual questions.

Questions of law might also arise in the context of a designation as covered critical infrastructure under the Cybersecurity Act of 2012. For example, the bill does not provide specific definitions for terms such as an "extraordinary number of fatalities" or "prolonged absence." The bill would also prohibit the Secretary from designating a commercial information technology product, or any services provided in support of a commercial information technology product, as covered critical infrastructure.[73] Questions of interpretation may arise with respect to this exemption. For example, the Secretary may wish to designate a larger system, which happens to contain a commercial information technology product, as covered critical infrastructure. However, the affected entity may argue that such a designation would violate the bill's prohibition on designating commercial information technology products as covered critical infrastructure. If the Secretary were to interpret these provisions as permitting that designation, perhaps arguing that there is a distinction between designating a commercial information technology product as critical

---

[67] Owners of critical infrastructure can also self-designate or request that their systems or assets be considered covered critical infrastructure. S. 2105, §103(b)(4).

[68] S. 2105, §103(b)(1)(C).

[69] S. 2105, §103(b)(1)(C)(ii).

[70] That term is defined in the bill to mean "a commercial item that organizes or communicates information electronically." S. 2105, §2(1).

[71] S. 2105, §103(b)(2).

[72] S. 2105, §103(c). Many other Secretarial decisions, such as the determination that an existing regulatory scheme is inadequate, would appear to have sufficient judicially manageable standards to qualify for judicial review under the APA. *But see* S. 2105, §104(f)(1), authorizing the President to exempt any covered critical infrastructure from performance standards, if the President determines that a sector specific regulatory agency has sufficient requirements to protect against the identified risks. Such a decision may not be subject to judicial review because the APA does not generally apply to decisions made by the President. Franklin v. Massachusetts, 505 U.S. 788, 800 (1992).

[73] S. 2105, §103(c).

---

infrastructure and designating a system that is partially comprised of a commercial information technology product as covered critical infrastructure, it is likely that a reviewing court would evaluate this interpretation under the *Chevron* analysis described above. Specifically, a reviewing court would first ask whether the statute clearly answered the question, and, if the statute did not, would uphold the Secretary's interpretation to the extent that it is a reasonable one.

In order to enforce its provisions, the Cybersecurity Act of 2012 explicitly authorizes DHS to develop civil monetary penalties to be levied against covered critical infrastructure that was found to be noncompliant with the applicable performance standards.[74] The bill would allow owners or operators of covered critical infrastructure to self-certify annually that they are compliant, or submit to a third-party assessment of compliance.[75] However, audits and inspections by DHS would also be authorized if there were a reasonable suspicion of noncompliance.[76]

With respect to private civil liability, the Cybersecurity Act of 2012 provides some immunity for covered critical infrastructure that experience cybersecurity incidents related to identified risks.[77] The owner or operator of the covered critical infrastructure would be eligible to receive immunity from punitive damages in a private civil suit, but such immunity would be available if the entity had also met applicable performance requirements under the bill, had received a successful assessment, and was also in substantial compliance at the time of the incident.[78]

The Cybersecurity Act of 2012 would authorize the Secretary of Homeland Security to collect information from covered critical infrastructure in order to conduct risk assessments and to evaluate compliance with applicable performance standards.[79] The bill provides that any information collected under its authority would be considered critical infrastructure information (CII) under the Critical Infrastructure Information Act of 2002 (CIIA).[80] While information must normally be submitted voluntarily in order to be considered CIIA, the Cybersecurity Act of 2012 removes this requirement with respect to information that would be collected pursuant to the bill.[81] Information would not be considered CII if it were submitted to conceal violations of law, inefficiency, or administrative error; prevent embarrassment to a person, organization, or agency; or interfere with competition in the private sector.[82]

In addition to the authorities established under Title I of the Cybersecurity Act of 2012, Title III of the bill would amend the Homeland Security Act of 2002 to create a National Center for Cybersecurity and Communications (NCCC or Center).[83] The NCCC is charged with managing

---

[74] S. 2105, §105(c)(1)(B).

[75] S. 2105, §105(c)(1)(A). Companies that can demonstrate that their covered critical infrastructure are sufficiently secured against the risks identified would only have to certify every three years. S. 2105, §105(c)(4).

[76] S. 2105, §105(d)(2).

[77] S. 2105, §105(e).

[78] *Id.*

[79] S. 2105, §§101(b), 105(d)(3)(A), 107(a)(1).

[80] S. 2105, §107(b). The CIIA consists of a group of provisions that address the circumstances under which the Department of Homeland Security may obtain, use, and disclose critical infrastructure information as part of a critical infrastructure protection program. It was enacted, in part, to respond to the need for the federal government and owners and operators of the nation's critical infrastructures to share information on vulnerabilities and threats, and to promote information sharing between the private and public sectors in order to protect critical assets.

[81] S. 2105, §107(b).

[82] S. 2105, §107(a)(2).

[83] S. 2105 §301 (new HSA §242(a)).

"Federal efforts to secure, protect, and ensure the resiliency of the Federal information infrastructure, national information infrastructure, and national security and emergency preparedness communications infrastructure...."[84] The Director of the NCCC will be appointed by the President and will report directly to the Secretary of Homeland Security (the Secretary).[85] Additionally, the NCCC will have one deputy director from the intelligence community[86] who is chosen by the Director of National Intelligence and reports directly to the Secretary.[87]

There are several places in which Title I provisions detailing DHS's authority to regulate critical infrastructure security overlap with the Center's responsibilities as outlined in Title III. For example, both the Center and the Secretary of Homeland Security are instructed to conduct cyber risk assessments of critical infrastructure,[88] and inform critical infrastructure owners about security conditions. The Center must provide classified and unclassified security information to national information infrastructure owners, which could include entities designated as critical infrastructure by DHS under Title I.[89] DHS is required to provide information to critical infrastructure owners about cybersecurity threats, however, provision of classified information is not directly addressed.[90] Finally, both entities play a role in responding to cybersecurity emergencies. The Center must develop and coordinate a "national incident response plan that details the roles of Federal agencies, State and local governments, and the private sector...."[91] In similar language, DHS must "improve the capabilities and procedures of government and private section entities to respond to a major cyber incident" and "clarify specific roles, responsibilities, and authorities of the government" when responding.[92] Since these Title I and III authorities overlap but are not wholly duplicative, it may not be clear if or how the exercise of these authorities would coincide.

Title I also gives the President the authority to exempt organizations that have been designated as covered critical infrastructure by DHS from the requirements imposed in Title I, if they are sufficiently regulated by a sector-specific agency.[93] While these exempted entities are clearly free from Title I requirements, it appears that they are still subject to the Title III provisions that apply to covered critical infrastructure.[94] If they are not exempted, these information systems will be excepted from DHS requirements under Title I, but will still have to comply with the Title III

---

[84] *Id.* (new HSA §242(d)).

[85] *Id.* (new HSA §242(c)).

[86] *See Id.* (new HSA §241(12)). Intelligence community has the meaning given in 50 U.S.C. §401a(4), which includes the Office of Director of National Intelligence; the Central Intelligence Agency; the National Security Agency; certain elements of the Department of Defense; intelligence elements of the military branches, the Federal Bureau of Investigation, the Drug Enforcement Agency, and the Departments of Energy, State, Homeland Security, and Treasury.

[87] S. 2105 §301 (new HSA §242(g)(2)).

[88] S. 2105 §§102(a)(2), and 301 (new HSA §242(e)(2)).

[89] S. 2105 §301 (new HSA §242(e)(6)(B)).

[90] S. 2105 §105(b).

[91] S. 2105 §301 (new HSA §242(e)(8)).

[92] S. 2105 §109.

[93] S. 2105 §104(f).

[94] Title III defines covered critical infrastructure as "as system or asset designated by the Secretary ... in accordance with the procedure established under section 103 of the Cybersecurity Act of 2012." S. 2105 §301 (new HSA §241(3)). This definition makes no mention of the exemption process that takes place after the designation is determined, as laid out in Section 104. See S. 2105 §104(f).

affirmative obligation for covered critical infrastructure operators to share information with the Center about cyber incidents.[95]

Legal Issues Related to the Protection of Federal Networks

Prompted by a perceived threat to governmental information technology (IT) systems, DHS, in conjunction with the National Security Agency (NSA), has incrementally ramped up monitoring of federal government networks over the past decade to identify and prevent cyber attacks. A focal point of these efforts is EINSTEIN, a network intrusion system that monitors all federal agency networks for potential attacks. As part of this monitoring, all communications by federal executive agency employees made on federal networks, and incidentally, all communications they have with private citizens, are monitored for malicious activity. This monitoring may trigger Fourth Amendment guarantees to the right to be free from unreasonable searches and excessive government intrusion. Additionally, Congress has enacted statutory rules that place a higher restriction than the Constitution on government access to electronic communications.[96]

This section surveys EINSTEIN's background and discusses the Fourth Amendment concerns it raises for both federal employees and private citizen's communicating with them. It will then discuss alternative privacy and civil liberties protections that may be instituted to complement Fourth Amendment protections. Finally, this section discusses recent legislative efforts in the 112th Congress to improve the federal government's cybersecurity networks.

EINSTEIN Overview

Before EINSTEIN was introduced, federal agencies reported cyber threats to DHS manually and on an ad hoc basis.[97] It was usually done after the agency systems were affected by the attack. To remedy this, DHS, in collaboration with NSA, created EINSTEIN—a system to detect and report network intrusions. EINSTEIN's mandate derived from a combination of statutes, presidential directives, and agency memoranda. The first mandates for EINSTEIN came in 2002 with the Homeland Security Act and Homeland Security Presidential Directive 7.[98] In 2007, the Office of Management and Budget required all federal executive agencies to develop a comprehensive plan of action to defend against cyber threats.[99] Coinciding with these statutory and administrative directives, DHS and NSA launched EINSTEIN in three phases, each increasingly more sophisticated than the last.

---

[95] S. 2105 §301 (new HSA §243(c)(1)(B)).

[96] This section focuses on the constitutional concerns with EINSTEIN under the Fourth Amendment. Although statutes such as the Electronic Communications Privacy Act of 1986, P.L. 99-508, 100 Stat. 1848, and the Privacy Act of 1974, 5 U.S.C. §522a, may be implicated, they will not be discussed here.

[97] DEP'T OF HOMELAND SECURITY, PRIVACY IMPACT ASSESSMENT: EINSTEIN PROGRAM, at 3 (2004) (hereinafter EINSTEIN 1 PRIVACY IMPACT ASSESSMENT), available at http://www.dhs.gov/xlibrary/assets/privacy/privacy_pia_eisntein.pdf.

[98] *Id.* at 1.

[99] Office of Management and Budget, Memorandum for the Heads of Executive Departments and Agencies: Implementation of Trusted Internet Connections (TIC) (November 20, 2007), available at http://www.whitehouse.gov/ sites/default/files/omb/assets/omb/memoranda/fy2008/m08-05.pdf.

DHS rolled out EINSTEIN 1 in 2004 to automate the process by which federal agencies reported cyber threats to the United States Computer Emergency Readiness Team (US-CERT), the operational arm of DHS's cybersecurity division.[100] Under EINSTEIN 1, federal agencies voluntarily sent "flow records" of Internet network activity to DHS so it could monitor the Internet traffic across the federal .gov domain. These flow records included basic routing information such as the IP addresses of the connecting computer and the federal computer connected to.[101] US-CERT used this information to detect and mitigate malicious activity that threatened federal networks. This information was shared with both public and private actors on the DHS website.[102]

In an effort to upgrade EINSTEIN's capabilities, DHS launched EINSTEIN 2, which is capable of alerting US-CERT of malicious network intrusions in near-real time.[103] Sensors installed at all federal agency Internet access points make a copy of all network activity coming to and from federal networks, including addressing information and the content of the communication.[104] These data are later scanned for the presence of "signatures," patterns that correspond to a known threat, such as denial of service attacks, network backdoors, malware, worms, Trojan horses, and routing anomalies.[105] The system triggers an alert when it senses malicious activity. All the data corresponding with the trigger, including the content of the communication, are saved.[106] Personnel at US-CERT then analyze the stored messages and act accordingly.

In 2010, DHS began testing EINSTEIN 3 on one federal agency.[107] In addition to *detecting* cyber threats, this newest iteration also is designed to *block* and *respond* to these threats before any harm is done.[108] US-CERT is also testing the ability of EINSTEIN 3 to provide real-time information sharing with other federal agencies and the NSA.[109]

EINSTEIN and the Fourth Amendment

There is no doubt that EINSTEIN's monitoring of all communications coming to and from federal agency computers poses significant privacy implications—a concern acknowledged by DHS, interest groups, academia, and the general public.[110] This program affects not only federal

---

[100] EINSTEIN 1 PRIVACY IMPACT ASSESSMENT, *supra* note 94 at 4.

[101] *Id.* at 6-7. An IP address is a unique identifier used by most computers when sending data over the Internet. It is akin to a personal telephone number or street address. *See* Stephanie Crawford, *What is an IP address?*, HOW STUFF WORKS, http://computer howstuffworks.com/internet/basics/question549 htm.

[102] See http://www.us-cert.gov/cas/techalerts/ for an example of cybersecurity alerts provided to the public.

[103] DEP'T OF HOMELAND SECURITY, PRIVACY IMPACT ASSESSMENT: EINSTEIN 2, at 1 (2008) (hereinafter EINSTEIN 2 PRIVACY IMPACT ASSESSMENT), available at http://www.dhs.gov/xlibrary/assets/privacy/privacy_pia_einstein2.pdf.

[104] *Id.* at 9. For more information on intrusion detection systems, see NAT'L INSTITUTE OF STANDARDS AND TECH., GUIDE TO INTRUSION DETECTION AND PREVENTION SYSTEMS (IDPS) (2007) (Pub. No. 800-94), available at http://csrc nist.gov/publications/nistpubs/800-94/SP800-94.pdf (hereinafter "NIST REPORT").

[105] NIST REPORT, *supra* note 101, at 9-5.

[106] EINSTEIN 2 PRIVACY IMPACT ASSESSMENT, *supra* note 100, at 10.

[107] According to DHS, the name of the agency is classified. DEP'T OF HOMELAND SECURITY, PRIVACY IMPACT ASSESSMENT: INITIATIVE THREE EXERCISE, at 3 (2010) (hereinafter EINSTEIN 3 PRIVACY IMPACT ASSESSMENT) available at http://www.dhs.gov/xlibrary/assets/privacy/privacy_pia_nppd_initiative3.pdf.

[108] *Id.* at 3.

[109] *Id.* at 4.

[110] *See, e.g.*, DEP'T OF HOMELAND SECURITY, PRIVACY COMPLIANCE REVIEW OF THE EINSTEIN PROGRAM (2012) (continued...)

---

employees, but also any private citizen who communicates with them. DHS has developed a set of procedures to address these concerns, such as minimization of information collection, training and accountability requirements, and retention rules. Notwithstanding these steps, growth of this Internet monitoring program may trigger privacy interests protected under the Fourth Amendment.

The Fourth Amendment provides in relevant part: "The right of the people to be secure in their persons, houses, papers, and effects, against unreasonable searches and seizures, shall not be violated...."[111] The principal purpose of the Fourth Amendment is to protect the privacy of individuals against invasion from government officials.[112] Not all government acts, however, trigger Fourth Amendment protections. For the Fourth Amendment to apply, a court must first inquire whether the governmental act constitutes a *search* or *seizure* in the constitutional sense.[113] To determine if a *search* has occurred, a court will ask whether the individual had an actual expectation of privacy that society would deem reasonable.[114] If yes, the court will then ask if the search was reasonable—the core Fourth Amendment requirement.[115] Except in well-defined instances, a search is not reasonable unless the government obtains a warrant based upon probable cause.[116] There are, however, exceptions to this rule such as special needs and consent that will be explored below.

There seems to be a consensus in federal courts that Internet users are not entitled to privacy in the non-content, routing information of their Internet communications.[117] In *United States v. Forrester*, the government obtained court permission to install a device similar to a pen register to record the to/from addresses of the defendant's emails, the IP addresses of the sites he visited, and the total volume of data sent to and from his account.[118] The Ninth Circuit Court of Appeals held that these surveillance techniques were indistinguishable from the pen register upheld by the

---

(...continued)

(hereinafter EINSTEIN PRIVACY COMPLIANCE REVIEW), available at http://www.dhs.gov/xlibrary/assets/privacy/privacy_privcomrev_nppd_ein.pdf; THE CONSTITUTION PROJECT, RECOMMENDATIONS FOR THE IMPLEMENTATION OF A COMPREHENSIVE AND CONSTITUTIONAL CYBERSECURITY POLICY (2012) (hereinafter THE CONSTITUTION PROJECT), available at http://www.constitutionproject.org/pdf/TCPCybersecurityReport.pdf; Jack Goldsmith, *The Cyberthreat, Government Network Operations, and the Fourth Amendment* (2010), available at http://www.brookings.edu/papers/2010/1208_4th_amendment_goldsmith.aspx.

[111] U.S. CONST. amend. IV.

[112] Camara v. Mun. Ct., 387 U.S. 523, 528 (1967).

[113] Kyllo v. United States, 533 U.S. 27, 32-33 (2001).

[114] This formulation for determining whether a search of seizure occurred derives from Justice Harlan's concurrence in *Katz v. United States*, 389 U.S. 347, 361 (1967) (Harlan, J., concurring).

[115] Texas v. Brown, 460 U.S. 730, 739 (1983).

[116] Mincey v. United States, 437 U.S. 385, 390 (1978). Probable cause has been defined as "the facts and circumstances within the officers' knowledge and of which they had reasonably trustworthy information are sufficient in themselves to warrant a man of reasonable caution in the belief that an offense has been or is being committed." Brinegar v. United States, 338 U.S. 160, 175 (1948).

[117] United States v. Forrester, 512 F.3d 500, 511 (9th Cir. 2007) (holding no reasonable expectation of privacy in the to/from line addresses of e-mails and IP address of websites visited); United States v. Christie, 624 F.3d 558, 574 (3rd Cir.) (holding no reasonable expectation of privacy in IP address); United States v. Perrine, 518 F.3d 1196, 1205 (10th Cir.) (holding no reasonable expectation of privacy in Internet subscriber information given to Internet service provider).

[118] United States v. Forrester, 512 F.3d at 511. A pen register is a device that records the numbers dialed from a telephone. 18 U.S.C. §3127(3).

Supreme Court in *Smith v. Maryland*.[119] Internet users should be aware, the panel reasoned, that this routing information is provided to the Internet service provider for the purpose of directing the information.[120]

On the other hand, the cases generally demonstrate that an individual has a legitimate expectation of privacy in the *content* of a communication. In *United States v. Warshak*, the Ninth Circuit ruled that a "subscriber enjoys a reasonable expectation of privacy in the contents of emails that are stored with, or sent or received through, a commercial ISP."[121] In an earlier case, the Second Circuit opined that Internet users have an expectation of privacy in the content of the e-mail while in transmission.[122] Although the Supreme Court declined to resolve this issue in *City of Ontario v. Quon*, deciding the case on other grounds, it opined in dicta that "cell phones and text message communications are so pervasive that some persons may consider them to be an essential means or necessary instruments for self-expression, even self-identification. That might strengthen the case for an expectation of privacy."[123]

This content/non-content distinction is as old as Fourth Amendment case law.[124] In the late nineteenth century, the Court explained in *Ex parte Jackson* that the outside of a mailed letter—its "outward form and weight"—was not entitled constitutional protection.[125] However, the government must obtain a warrant before examining the contents of a letter or sealed package.[126] The Court protected the inside contents of the letter, but held that the outside, non-content material was not entitled to (in modern parlance) a reasonable expectation of privacy. This same rule was carried over to the telephone context.[127] In *Katz v. United States*, the Court held that the contents of Katz's conversation—the actual words spoken—were protected under the Fourth Amendment.[128] A decade later the Court completed the other side of the doctrine in *Smith v. Maryland*, and held that a person has no expectation of privacy in the non-content, routing information of the telephone call—the numbers dialed.[129]

---

[119] *Id.* at 510. In *Smith v. Maryland*, the Court held that the use of a pen register—a device that obtains the telephone numbers dialed from a certain phone—was not a search under the Fourth Amendment. 442 U.S. 735, 745-46 (1979).

[120] *Forrester*, 512 F.3d at 510.

[121] United States v. Warshak, 631 F.3d 266, 287 (6th Cir. 2010) (internal quotation marks omitted).

[122] United States v. Lifshitz, 369 F.3d 173, 190 (2d Cir. 2004).

[123] City of Ontario v. Quon, 130 S. Ct. 2619, 2630 (2010).

[124] *See* Orin Kerr, *Applying the Fourth Amendment to the Internet: A General Approach*, 62 STAN. L. REV. 1005, 1022-29) (2010) (analogizing the content/non-content distinction developed in the Fourth Amendment letter and telephone cases with Internet communications).

[125] *Ex parte* Jackson, 96 U.S. 727, 733 (1878); *Forrester*, 512 F.3d at 511 (citing *Ex parte* Jackson, 96 U.S. at 733).

[126] *Ex parte* Jackson, 96 U.S. at 733.

> The constitutional guaranty of the right of the people to be secure in their papers against unreasonable searches and seizures extends to their papers, thus closed against inspection, wherever they may be. Whilst in the mail, they can only be opened and examined under like warrant, issued upon similar oath or affirmation, particularly describing the thing to be seized, as is required when papers are subjected to search in one's own household. No law of Congress can place in the hands of officials connected with the postal service any authority to invade the secrecy of letters and such sealed packages in the mail; and all regulations adopted as to mail matter of this kind must be in subordination to the great principle embodied in the fourth amendment of the Constitution.

Id.

[127] Kerr, *supra* note 121, at 1023-24.

[128] Katz v. United States, 389 U.S. 347, 359 (1967)

[129] Smith v. Maryland, 442 U.S. 735, 745-46 (1979).

EINSTEIN 2 not only collects the routing, non-content portions of communications, such as e-mail header information, but also scans and collects the content of the communications, such as the body of e-mails.[130] Based on the reasoning of the Internet content cases, individuals most likely have a reasonable expectation of privacy in those electronic communications.[131] The EINSTEIN program requires a Fourth Amendment inquiry into two discrete classes of individuals: (1) federal agency employees who access federal networks while at work; and (2) private persons who either contact a federal agency directly or who communicate via the Internet with a federal employee.[132] The Fourth Amendment rights of the former primarily rest on cases dealing with privacy in the workplace and consent, while the latter requires a broader look at privacy and electronic communications.

Monitoring Communications from Federal Employees

As work and personal lives can become enmeshed, many employees are accessing not only work e-mail while on the clock, but also personal e-mails. EINSTEIN monitors not only federal executive agency employees' work e-mails or other official Internet activity, but also any information accessed on a federal agency computer including personal e-mails accessed from sites such as Gmail or Hotmail, or other Internet communications such as Facebook and Twitter. This poses several Fourth Amendment issues.

In *City of Ontario v. Quon*, the Supreme Court upheld under the Fourth Amendment the city's search of text messages sent on a city-issued pager by a police officer employed by that city.[133] Before issuing the pagers, the city had announced a usage policy that informed the officers that the city reserved the right to monitor the use of the pager including e-mail and Internet use, with or without notice to the employee.[134] The Court assumed without deciding that the employee had a reasonable expectation of privacy in the sent text messages, that the review of text messages constituted a search, and that the same rules that apply to a search of an employee's office apply equally to an intrusion into his electronic communications.[135] Further, the Court declined to decide which Fourth Amendment employment-based test from *O'Connor v. Ortega* applied—the plurality's "operational realities" test that looked at the specific facts of the employment situation on a case-by-case basis, or Justice Scalia's private employment equivalence test—because the Court decided the case on narrower grounds.[136]

---

[130] EINSTEIN PRIVACY COMPLIANCE REVIEW, *supra* note 107, at 5.

[131] *See* Legal Issues Relating to the Testing, Use, and Deployment of an Intrusion-Detection System (EINSTEIN 2.0) to Protect Unclassified Computer Networks in the Executive Branch, 33 Op. O.L.C. 1, *11 (2009) (hereinafter Legal Issues Relating to EINSTEIN 2.0), available at http://www.justice.gov/olc/2009/e2-issues.pdf.

[132] There is also a third category of cases: where a federal employee sends a communication while on the federal network to a private person. Because the principles that apply to communications from a private person to a federal employee are the same as the principles that apply to communications from a federal employee to a private person, these two categories will be discussed jointly.

[133] City of Ontario v. Quon, 130 S. Ct. 2619, 2624 (2010). For an in-depth treatment of *Quon*, see CRS Report R41344, *Public Employees' Right to Privacy in Their Electronic Communications: City of Ontario v. Quon in the Supreme Court* , by Charles Doyle.

[134] *Quon*, 130 S. Ct. at 2625.

[135] *Id.* at 2630.

[136] *Id.* at 2630.

The Court instead relied on the special needs exception to the warrant requirement, which holds that in certain limited instances a government employer need not get a warrant to conduct a search. When a government employer conducts a warrantless search for a "non-investigatory, work-related purpose," it does not violate the warrant requirement if it is "justified at its inception and if the measures are reasonably related to the objective of the search and not excessively intrusive in light of the circumstances giving rise to the search."[137] In the Court's judgment, the city had a "legitimate work-related rationale," and the scope of the search was reasonable and not "excessively intrusive."[138]

Like the city communication policy in *Quon*, as a condition of enrolling in EINSTEIN 2, each federal agency is required to enter into an agreement with DHS that certifies that certain log-on banners or computer user agreements are used to ensure employees are aware of and consent to the monitoring, interception, and search of their communications on federal systems.[139] Applying the "operational realities" test from *O'Connor*, the Department of Justice's Office of Legal Counsel posits that use of the log-on banners on all federal computers will eliminate any expectation of privacy in communications transmitted over those systems.[140] Professor Orin Kerr takes a different approach, treating the terms of service of an Internet service contract—the equivalent to a log-on banner—as consent rather than an outright elimination of a reasonable expectation of privacy.[141] Under either approach, the conclusion reached is likely the same—the monitoring is in all likelihood reasonable.[142] However, *Quon* was limited to searches for a "noninvestigatory work-related purpose."[143] If EINSTEIN could be construed as overreaching this permissible purpose, say, by scanning e-mails for unlawful activity instead of simply malicious computer activity, a court may find its scope beyond *Quon*'s holding. Further, *Quon* insisted that these work-related investigations not be "excessively intrusive."[144] A reasonable argument could be made that monitoring the content of every employee communication is excessively intrusive. Additional questions remain. For instance, what is the scope of a non-investigatory, work-related purpose? Does scanning for malicious activity qualify as a work-related purpose? Does *United States v. Jones*'s physical intrusion test apply here where the employee's electronic *papers* and *effects* are being scanned?[145] Because no court has confronted a program like EINSTEIN, answers to these questions are unclear.

---

[137] *Id.* at 2631.

[138] *Id.* (internal citations omitted).

[139] Legal Issues Relating to EINSTEIN 2.0, *supra* note 128, at *11.

[140] *Id.* at 32-33.

[141] Kerr, *supra* note 121, at 1031.

[142] *See also* THE CONSTITUTION PROJECT, *supra* at note 107, at 14 ("For federal employees, the analysis that employees consent to having Einstein monitor communications is likely reasonable given the overwhelming importance of protecting key federal agency networks.").

[143] *Quon*, 130 S. Ct. at 2631.

[144] *Id.*

[145] Another possible approach is that taken in *United States v. Jones*, 565 U.S. ___ (2012) (slip op.), in which the Court held that a physical intrusion into a constitutionally protected area—there, the defendant's car (an effect)—coupled with an attempt to obtain information, was a Fourth Amendment search. If a court concluded that an e-mail is a paper (or packet of data, an effect), protected under the Fourth Amendment's catalog of protected areas (persons, houses, papers, and effects), the *Jones* physical intrusion analysis may call into question whether EINSTEIN's surveillance is constitutionally permissible.

Monitoring Communications from Private Persons to Federal Employees

EINSTEIN not only monitors the computer activity of federal agency employees, but also any communications sent by a private person to a federal employee on his governmental e-mail or personal e-mail. One may argue that these concerns are more serious than in the employment context, on the theory that there is neither a presumption that an individual's privacy rights are diminished nor has the private actor consented to monitoring by clicking on a log-on banner or user agreement that would inform him of the privacy implications of his communication.

Some would argue that the third-party doctrine permits EINSTEIN's monitoring of private parties.[146] Traditionally, there has been no Fourth Amendment protection for information voluntarily conveyed to a third-party.[147] This doctrine dates back to the "secret agent" cases, in which any words uttered to another person, including a government agent or informant, were not covered by the Fourth Amendment.[148] Because federal employees have agreed to permit governmental monitoring of their communications, the Office of Legal Counsel (OLC) argues they are permitting *ex ante* surveillance of all their communications, including those from private persons to the federal employee's personal e-mail.[149]

However, the third-party cases have traditionally applied only to non-content information. In *Smith v. Maryland*, the Court noted that pen registers only disclose the telephone numbers dialed: "[n]either the purport of any communication between the caller and the recipient of the call, their identities, nor whether the call was even completed is disclosed by pen registers."[150] The case rested on the devices "limited capabilities."[151] The Ninth Circuit borrowed this reasoning in *Forrester*, where the panel distinguished "mere addressing" in an e-mail such as the to/from line, from "more content-rich information" such as the text in the body of an e-mail.[152] And as noted in *United States v. Warshak*, people still should expect privacy in the content of their telephone calls despite the ability of an operator to listen.[153] Further, the Supreme Court has noted that "the broad and unsuspected governmental incursions into conversational privacy which electronic surveillance entails necessitate the application of Fourth Amendment safeguards."[154] These cases severely diminish the argument that the third-doctrine permits absolute access to private communications. Instead, it could be reasonable to conclude from these cases that the third-party doctrine would permit access to the routing information of Internet communications, but might not go so far as to allow monitoring of the content of those communications.

---

[146] Legal Issues Relating to EINSTEIN 2.0, *supra* note 128, at 35-36 (citing Smith v. Maryland, 442 U.S. 735, 743-44) (1979).

[147] *United States v. Miller*, 425 U.S. 435 (1976) holding that financial statements and deposit slips transmitted to bank were not protected from police inquiry because they had been turned over to a third party); *Smith*, 442 U.S. 735. It should be noted that in *United States v. Jones*, Justice Sotomayor opined that it "may be necessary to reconsider the premise that an individual has no reasonable expectation of privacy in information voluntarily disclosed to third parties." United States v. Jones, 565 U.S. ___, 5 (Sotomayor, J., concurring in the judgment and the opinion).

[148] United States v. White, 401 U.S. 745, 750 (1971) (holding that the Fourth Amendment "affords no protection to a wrongdoer's misplaced belief that a person to whom he voluntarily confides his wrongdoing will not reveal it.") (internal quotation marks omitted).

[149] Legal Issues Relating to EINSTEIN 2.0, *supra* note 128, at 36-37.

[150] *Smith*, 442 U.S. at 741 (quoting United States v. N.Y. Tel. Co., 434 U.S. 159, 167 (1977)).

[151] *Id.* at 742.

[152] United States v. Forrester, 512 F.3d 500, 511 (9th Cir. 2007).

[153] United States v. Warshak, 631 F.3d 266, 285 (6th Cir. 2007).

[154] United States v. U.S. Dist. Ct., 407 U.S. 297, 313 (1972).

Additionally, the OLC contends that under the "secret agent" cases the government can monitor private communications even if the sender is unaware that the recipient is a federal employee or did not anticipate that the communication would be opened on a federal computer.[155] The "secret agent" cases generally hold that "when a person communicates to third-party even on the understanding that the communication is confidential, he cannot object if the third party conveys that information or records thereof to law enforcement authorities."[156] Because these cases do not limit the instances this rule can be applied, it seems reasonable that they can be applied to EINSTEIN.

Alternative to Traditional Warrant Requirement

Assuming both federal employees and those communicating with them have a reasonable expectation of privacy in the contents of their communications, EINSTEIN must be tested under the general reasonableness requirement of the Fourth Amendment. A search is generally unreasonable without a warrant or some individualized suspicion.[157] However, under the "special needs exception" cases, the Court has held that when there are special governmental needs, beyond normal law enforcement, the government may need neither a warrant nor any level of individualized suspicion.[158] To determine whether the special needs exception applies, the Court balances the individual's privacy expectations against the governmental interest at stake.[159] This rule has been used to support certain police searches at checkpoints such as sobriety roadblocks,[160] border searches,[161] and checkpoints looking for a witness to a crime.[162] However, the Court did not permit a drug interdiction checkpoint when the "primary purpose was to detect evidence of ordinary criminal wrongdoing."[163]

Here, an argument could be made that the nature of cybersecurity and the impracticability of obtaining a warrant might justify application of the special needs doctrine to the EINSTEIN program.[164] The ostensible primary purpose of the program's cybersecurity measures is not for ordinary law enforcement needs, but instead to protect the critical infrastructure of the nation. Moreover, the government will need to act quickly if the program is to be feasible.[165] It could also be argued, however, that unless the threat required immediate review, a government agency should obtain a warrant based upon probable cause to review personally identifiable information, or, at a minimum, review the communications in a redacted format that includes only the threat information and no personally identifiable information.[166] As one commentator noted, it is nearly

---

[155] Legal Issues Relating to EINSTEIN 2.0, *supra* note 128, at 39.

[156] SEC v. Jerry T. O'Brien, Inc., 467 U.S. 735, 743 (1984).

[157] Chandler v. Miller, 520 U.S. 305, 308 (1997).

[158] Nat'l Treasury Emplys. Union v. Von Raab, 489 U.S. 656, 665-66 (1989).

[159] *Id.*

[160] Michigan Dep't of State Police v. Sitz, 496 U.S. 444, 455 (1990).

[161] United States v. Ramsey, 431 U.S. 606 (1977).

[162] Illinois v. Lidster, 540 U.S. 419, 428 (2004).

[163] City of Indianapolis v. Edmond, 531 U.S. 32, 38 (2000).

[164] Legal Issues Relating to EINSTEIN 2.0, *supra* note 128, at 54.

[165] Goldsmith, *supra* note 107, at 14.

[166] THE CONSTITUTION PROJECT, *supra* note 107, at 16.

impossible to predict what is reasonable without knowing the severity of the cybersecurity threat and the exact measures taken to meet it.[167]

Privacy and Civil Liberties Oversight

In addition to the Fourth Amendment, there may be other mechanisms for protecting the privacy of Internet users. Indeed, the Constitution is only the floor for privacy protections. In many instances, Congress and state legislatures have created privacy protections beyond what is protected under their respective constitutions. These include statutes such as the Electronic Communications Privacy Act[168] and the Privacy Act of 1974.[169]

As to existing privacy protections, EINSTEIN has several privacy safeguards. For example, federal agencies are required to post notices on their websites that computer security information is being collected.[170] The computer programs recording network flow records strip down the information so that minimal content information is exposed.[171] Further, only the raw computer network traffic that contains malicious activity is viewed by DHS personnel; any "clean" traffic is promptly deleted from the system.[172] Information is only collected when it relates to an actual cyber threat.[173] Analysts handling the monitored communications are given privacy training on an annual basis.[174] These privacy protections are handled internally within DHS.

Jack Goldsmith, former head of the Office of Legal Counsel, has proposed a system of four oversight mechanisms similar to the Foreign Intelligence Surveillance Court[175] to ensure the reasonableness of the searches under EINSTEIN: (1) independent *ex ante* scrutiny to ensure that the governmental procedures stay within their statutory authority; (2) privacy protections such as minimization procedures, also subject to *ex ante* judicial review; (3) *ex post* oversight mechanisms, in which the Attorney General and the Director of National Intelligence report to Congress every six months regarding privacy compliance and the inspectors general from each agency also report to Congress on a yearly basis; and (4) a sunset provision requiring Congress to reapprove the regime four years into operation.[176]

Others have proposed there be some form of independent oversight beyond DHS's privacy office.[177] Additionally, there are proposals that content of communications not be shared with law

---

[167] Goldsmith, *supra* note 107, at 13.

[168] Electronic Communications Privacy Act of 1986, P.L. 99-508, 100 Stat. 1848.

[169] Privacy Act of 1974, P.L. 93-579, 88 Stat. 1896.

[170] EINSTEIN 1 PRIVACY IMPACT ASSESSMENT, *supra* note 94, at 9.

[171] EINSTEIN 2 PRIVACY IMPACT ASSESSMENT, *supra* note 100, at 12.

[172] *Id.*

[173] EINSTEIN PRIVACY COMPLIANCE REVIEW, *supra* note 107, at 4.

[174] *Id.* at 7.

[175] The Foreign Intelligence Surveillance Court is a comprised of 11 federal district court judges who are designated by the Chief Justice to hear applications for surveillance orders authorized under the Foreign Intelligence Surveillance Act of 1978. 50 U.S.C. §1803.

[176] Goldsmith, *supra* note 107, at 14.

[177] THE CONSTITUTION PROJECT, *supra* note 107, at 28.

enforcement officials or used in any non-cyber crime investigation, unless the data was obtained as part of a legitimate cybersecurity threat.[178]

Legislation in the 112th Congress

This section provides a brief description of proposed cybersecurity legislation in the 112th Congress that include provisions regarding the EINSTEIN program with particular emphasis placed on the provisions that implicate the legal issues discussed above.

S. 2105, Cybersecurity Act of 2012

S. 2105, the Cybersecurity Act of 2012 was introduced on February 14, 2012. Title II of the bill would amend the Federal Information Security Management Act (FISMA) to codify many of the current executive agency network intrusion practices described above. Specifically, the bill would enact a new Section 3553 of Title 44 of the United States Code to provide the Secretary of DHS with the statutory authority to oversee all information security policies that will be binding on all federal agencies.[179] The Secretary would be given the explicit statutory authority to "acquire, intercept, retain, use, and disclose communications and other system traffic that are transiting to or from or store on agency information systems and deploy countermeasures with regard to the communications and system traffic." In light of the test phase of EINSTEIN 3, this section apparently would vest in the Secretary the authority to not only intercept communications, but to react to actionable data based on perceived threats. Consistent with current practice, The Cybersecurity Act of 2012 would leave the Department of Defense (DOD), the Central Intelligence Agency (CIA), and the Office of the Director of National Intelligence in charge of their respective network intrusion systems. This bill would also permit DHS to contract with private ISPs to further its mission of preventing network intrusions.

Additionally, the National Center for Cybersecurity and Communications (NCCC) created under Title III of the Cybersecurity Act of 2012[180] would have various responsibilities with respect to federal networks. First, the NCCC must implement and enforce a security system for the federal information infrastructure,[181] which does not include national security systems or information systems used by the Department of Defense, the military or the intelligence community.[182] Second, the Center is to provide cybersecurity technology, upon request, and information, both classified and unclassified, to owners of national information infrastructure. Third, the NCCC must develop a national incident response plan and is responsible for coordinating national cyber incident response efforts. Finally, the NCCC must create an information sharing system that collects information from and redistributes information to federal agencies, state and local governments, national information infrastructure, critical infrastructure, and the private sector. Both federal agencies and critical infrastructure have an affirmative obligation to provide certain

---

[178] *Id.*

[179] S. 2105, 112th Cong. §3553 (2012).

[180] S. 2105 §301 (new HSA §242(a)).

[181] "Federal information infrastructure" is defined as "information and information systems that are owned, operated, controlled, or licensed by, or on behalf of, a Federal agency ... " but explicitly excludes systems used by the Department of Defense, the military, and an element of the intelligence community. S. 2105 §301 (new HSA §241(8)).

[182] *Id.* (new HSA §241(8)(B), 242(e)(3)).

information to the Center's information sharing program.[183] Other entities, including state and local governments and private sector actors, can participate voluntarily in the program.[184]

Title III instructs the NCCC to "develop, oversee the implementation of, and enforce policies, principles, and guidelines on information security for the federal information infrastructure, including exercise of the authorities under the Federal Information Security Management Act of 2002."[185] Therefore, it appears that NCCC is intended to exercise the authority granted to the Secretary in Title II.

Several provisions in Title III also appear to overlap with authority granted to DHS under FISMA in Title II. For example, both Title II and Title III require risk assessments to be completed on agency information systems. In Title III, NCCC must conduct risk assessments on all federal information systems, which excludes national security systems and systems used by the Department of Defense, the military, or the Intelligence Community.[186] In Title II, DHS is instructed to conduct risk assessments on agency information systems, except national security systems and systems used by the Department of Defense, the Central Intelligence Agency (CIA), and the Office of the Director of National Intelligence (DNI).[187]

Additionally, the security policies and procedures created under Title II and Title III appear to apply to different sets of federal agencies because of different exemptions granted under each Title. While national security systems and systems used by the Department of Defense, CIA, and DNI are exempted from the security policies and procedures implemented by DHS pursuant to Title II, other members of the intelligence community are not exempted.[188] In contrast, all national security systems and systems used by the Department of Defense, the military, and the entire Intelligence Community are exempted from the requirements NCCC must implement under Title III.[189] Therefore, it appears that the NCCC may be implementing two different sets of policies for two different sets of federal agencies, one set under Title II and one set under Title III.

It appears that all federal agencies must participate in the NCCC information sharing system, including complying with the affirmative obligation to provide information to the Center.[190]

H.R. 3674, Promoting and Enhancing Cybersecurity and Information Sharing Effectiveness Act of 2012 (PRECISE Act)

H.R. 3674, the Promoting and Enhancing Cybersecurity and Information Sharing Effectiveness Act of 2012 (PRECISE Act) was introduced on December 15, 2011. As introduced, H.R. 3674 did not expressly address federal efforts to implement and strengthen the EINSTEIN program. However, on April 18, 2012, the House Committee on Homeland Security held a mark up of the bill and agreed to an amendment that would codify DHS's EINSTEIN program.

---

[183] *Id.* (new HSA §243(b)(1)(B), (c)(1)(B)).

[184] *Id.* (new HSA §243(c)(1)(C)).

[185] *Id.* (new HSA §242(e)(3)).

[186] *Id.* (new HSA §242(e)(2)).

[187] *Id.* §201 (new 44 U.S.C. §3553(b)(3), (f)).

[188] *See Id.* (new 44 U.S.C. §3553(f)).

[189] *See* S. 2105 §301 (new HSA §241(8)) (defining "Federal information infrastructure").

[190] *Id.* (new HSA §243(b)(2)(B)-(C)).

H.R. 3674, as amended, would expressly permit DHS to "acquire, intercept, retain, use, and disclose communications" coming to or from any federal computer and to deploy countermeasures against potential malicious activity.[191] This is a codification of EINSTEIN 3's interception and response system tested on one agency by DHS in 2010.[192] Under this bill, an interception or countermeasure[193] must be "reasonably necessary" for protecting the federal system against a cybersecurity threat.[194] DHS may only retain the information to protect the federal systems against attack or to mitigate future attacks. The intercepted information may be used for law enforcement purposes, but only if authorized by the Attorney General.

Under this bill, notice must be provided to users of federal systems concerning the potential interception or use of their communication. Generally, this will take the form of a log-on banner for federal employees[195] or a federal website privacy policy page.[196] What is unclear, however, is whether the disclaimer provision covers situations where a private person is communicating with a federal employee. In many instances, that person may not be informed by the federal agency that their communication is being monitored. As just discussed, the third-party doctrine may vitiate any Fourth Amendment protection in this communication such that a notice to a private person communicating with a federal computer is not necessary.[197] But again, the third party-doctrine has primarily been applied to non-content information.[198] H.R. 3674 does not distinguish between content and non-content communications, but permits interception of any communication that is "associated with a known or reasonably suspected cybersecurity threat."[199] As such, the Fourth Amendment may be applicable to the content-based information collected under the procedures established by H.R. 3674.

Additionally, DHS is permitted to contract with private entities that provide cybersecurity services in order to facilitate the interception and use of communications coming to and from federal computers.

H.R. 4257, Federal Information Security Amendments Act of 2012

H.R. 4257, the Federal Information Security Amendments Act of 2012 was introduced by Representatives Daryl Issa and Elijah Cummings on March 26, 2012. This bill would amend the Federal Information Security Management Act of 2002 (FISMA) to require all federal agencies to continuously monitor their computer networks for malicious activity—a codification of the EINSTEIN program—and would impose additional cybersecurity requirements of all federal

---

[191] H.R. 3674, 112th Cong. (2012) (new HSA §226(c)(1)).

[192] *See* EINSTEIN Overview, *supra* p. 14.

[193] The term "countermeasure" means "automated actions with defensive intent to modify or block data packets associated with electronic or wire communications, Internet traffic, program code, or other system traffic transiting to or from or stored on an information system for the purpose of protecting the information system from cybersecurity threats." H.R. 3674 (new HSA §226(g)(1)).

[194] *Id.* (new HSA §226(c)(1)(A)).

[195] Legal Issues Relating to EINSTEIN 2.0, *supra* note 128, at 14-15.

[196] *See* Department of Homeland Security, Web Site Privacy Policy, http://www.dhs.gov/xutil/gc_1157139158971.shtmm (last visited April 19, 2012).

[197] *See* United States v. Miller, 425 U.S. 435 (1976).

[198] Smith v. Maryland, 442 U.S. 735, 741 (1979).

[199] H.R. 3674 (new HSA §226(c)(1)(B)).

agencies.[200] Unlike the Lieberman-Feingold or Lungren bills, H.R. 4257 does not put control in the hands of DHS. Instead, the Office of Management and Budget (OMB) would oversee the implementation and requirements of information security policies.[201] In conjunction with the National Institute of Standards and Technology (NIST), OMB would create standards and guidelines for cybersecurity protection. The Director of OMB would be charged with ensuring agency compliance with these standards.

Under H.R. 4257, each federal agency would be responsible for "providing information security protections commensurate with the risk and magnitude of the harm resulting from unauthorized access, use, disclosure, disruption, modification or destruction of—(i) information collected or maintained by or on behalf of an agency; and (ii) information infrastructure used or operated by an agency or by a contractor of an agency or other organization on behalf of an agency; ..."[202] Each agency would be required to establish a chief information officer responsible for developing and overseeing the agencies information security program.

Additionally, OMB would be charged with establishing a federal information security incident center, which would act as a hub for federal cybersecurity systems. This center would, among other duties, provide assistance to agencies, compile and analyze information about cybersecurity incidents, and inform agencies about known cyber threats.[203]

Absent from H.R. 4257 are any express privacy or civil liberties protections. Potentially, these protections may be established in future guidelines created by NIST and OMB, but this is unclear from the language of the bill. Further, unlike H.R. 3674 (Lungren), there is no requirement that computer users be informed that their communications with a federal computer can be monitored. Absent from H.R. 4257 are any express privacy or civil liberties protections.

Legal Issues Related to Cybersecurity Threat Information Sharing

Many policymakers have argued that there is a need for the federal government and owners and operators of the nation's critical infrastructures to share information on vulnerabilities and threats, and to promote information sharing between the private and public sectors in order to protect critical assets from cybersecurity threats. Private sector entities may wish to share information with one another about threats they have faced or are currently facing. They may also wish to collaborate in devising solutions to these security issues. Additionally, the government may have information about cybersecurity threats that would be similarly useful to potential targets in the private sector. The government may also see value in having access to information from the private sector about cybersecurity threats.

Obstacles to information sharing may exist in current laws protecting electronic communications or in antitrust law. The Fourth Amendment, the Telecommunications Act of 1934, and state laws may also affect the legality of information sharing by the private sector. Entities that share

---

[200] H.R. 4257, 112th Cong. (2012) (new 44 U.S.C. §3554).

[201] *Id.* (new 44 U.S.C. §3553).

[202] *Id.* (new 44 U.S.C. §3554).

[203] *Id.* (new 44 U.S.C.§3555).

information may also be concerned that sharing or receiving such information may lead to civil and criminal liability, or that shared information may contain proprietary or confidential information that could be disclosed to competitors or government regulators.

Electronic Communications Privacy Act[204]

The Electronic Communications Privacy Act (ECPA) generally prohibits (1) the interception of wire, oral or electronic communications (wiretapping);[205] (2) access to the content of stored electronic communications and to communications transaction records;[206] and (3) the use of trap and trace devices and pen registers.[207]

ECPA generally prohibits intercepting wire, oral, or electronic communications by means of an electronic, mechanical or other device, but sets forth a number of exceptions to the general prohibition.[208] Relevant to this discussion, ECPA provides a general exemption for communications service providers, permitting them to intercept communications when incidental to "the rendition of service or the protection of the rights or the property of the provider of that service," or protecting themselves against fraud.[209] This exemption does not apply to random monitoring except where used for mechanical or service quality control checks. Communications service providers are also permitted to intercept communications in order to assist federal and state officials operating under a judicially supervised interception order,[210] and for the regulatory activities of the Federal Communications Commission.[211] In addition, communications service providers are permitted to intercept communications with customer consent.[212]

Under the stored communications provisions of ECPA, providers of electronic communication services (ECS) to the public may not disclose the contents of any "communication while in electronic storage by that service."[213] Public remote computer service (RCS) providers similarly may not disclose the contents of

> any communication which is carried or maintained on that service – (A) on behalf of, and received by means of electronic transmission from (or created by means of computer processing of communications received by means of electronic transmission from), a subscriber or customer of such service; (B) solely for the purpose of providing storage or

---

[204] See CRS Report 98-326, *Privacy: An Overview of Federal Statutes Governing Wiretapping and Electronic Eavesdropping*, by Gina Stevens and Charles Doyle for a more detailed discussion of the federal laws governing wiretapping and electronic eavesdropping, along with appendices including copies of the texts of ECPA and FISA. *See also* CRS Report R41733, *Privacy: An Overview of the Electronic Communications Privacy Act*, by Charles Doyle.

[205] 18 U.S.C. §§2510-2522.

[206] 18 U.S.C. §§2701-2712.

[207] 18 U.S.C. §§3121-3127. Pen registers capture the numbers dialed on a telephone line; trap and trace devices identify the originating number of a call on a particular phone line. *See* 18 U.S.C. §3127(3)-(4). The USA PATRIOT Act enlarged the coverage of the Pen Register Statute to include sender/addressee information relating to email and other forms of electronic communications. P.L. 107-56, §216(c)(2).

[208] 18 U.S.C. §2511.

[209] 18 U.S.C. §2511(2)(a)(i), (h).

[210] 18 U.S.C. §2511(2)(a)(ii).

[211] 18 U.S.C. §2511(2)(b).

[212] 18 U.S.C. §2511(2)(c).

[213] 18 U.S.C. §2702(a)(1).

---

computer processing services to such subscriber or customer, if the provider is not authorized to access the contents of any such communications for purposes of providing any services other than storage or computer processing.[214]

Both ECS and RCS providers may not disclose any "record or other information pertaining to a subscriber to or customer of such service (not including the contents of communications covered by [the disclosure restrictions described above]) to any government entity."[215]

However, the statute does provide a number of exceptions under which an ECS or RCS provider may disclose the contents of a communication. These exceptions cover disclosures made

- to the addressee or intended recipient of the communication;

- with the consent of the sender, addressee, or intended recipient of the communication, or to the subscriber in the case of remote computing service;

- in order to forward such communication to its destination;

- as may be necessarily incident to the rendition of the service or *to the protection of the rights or property of the service provider*;

- to the National Center for Missing and Exploited Children;

- to law enforcement if the contents were inadvertently obtained by the service provider and appear to pertain to the commission of a crime; and

- to a government entity, if the provider, in good faith, believes that an emergency involving danger of death or serious physical injury to any person requires disclosure.[216]

With respect to pen registers and trap and trace devices, ECPA outlaws installation or use of a pen register or trap and trace device, except under one of seven circumstances:

- pursuant to a court order issued under sections 3121-3127 (pen registers and trap and trace devices);

- pursuant to a Foreign Intelligence Surveillance Act (FISA) court order;[217]

- with the consent of the user;

- when incidental to service;

- when necessary to protect users from abuse of service;

- when necessary to protect providers from abuse of service;[218] or

- in an emergency situation.[219]

---

[214] 18 U.S.C. §2702(a)(2).

[215] 18 U.S.C. §2702(a)(3).

[216] 18 U.S.C. §2702(b) (emphasis added). The record disclosure exceptions are similar. 18 U.S.C. 2702(c).

[217] 18 U.S.C. §3121 ("Except as provided in this section, no person may install or use a pen register or a trap and trace device without first obtaining a court order under section 3123 of this title or under the Foreign Intelligence Surveillance Act of 1978 (50 U.S.C. 1801 et seq.)").

[218] 18 U.S.C. §3121(b).

[219] 18 U.S.C. §3125(a).

Some have argued that the framework provided by ECPA may be an obstacle to sharing cyber threat information among communications service providers or between such entities and the government,[220] and may prevent them from acting to protect their customers and networks. The statute permits service providers to conduct random monitoring of communications in order to perform mechanical or service quality control checks; however, these purposes may not sufficiently capture the wholesale monitoring of networks to detect or intercept cyber threats.[221] Additionally, the restrictions on voluntary disclosures of the contents of communications and addressing information are generally limited to the purpose of protecting the service provider's rights or property. Consequently, ECPA may hinder sharing of information about cyber threats where the service provider is not the target of the threat. Given this uncertainty, providers may be hesitant to share cyber threat information as violating ECPA can expose them to criminal penalties and private civil liability.

Antitrust Law

Companies may be assisted in combating cybersecurity threats by sharing information with one another about threats they have faced or are currently facing. Companies may also wish to collaborate in devising solutions to these security issues. The antitrust laws are often cited as an impediment to such collaboration. This is so because if a collaboration is found to violate antitrust laws, the collaborating entities may be subject to civil and criminal penalties.[222]

Section 1 of the Sherman Antitrust Act prohibits contracts, combinations, and conspiracies in restraint of trade.[223] The Supreme Court has found that not all contracts or combinations that restrain trade are forbidden by the Sherman Act; rather, only those agreements that unreasonably restrain trade are prohibited.[224] Nonetheless, when competitors share information with one another, concerns regarding violations of the antitrust laws may arise.[225] The sharing of information may create the opportunity to conspire to fix prices, restrain output, or otherwise agree to unreasonably restrain competition to the detriment of consumers.

Two types of analyses are used to determine the lawfulness of collaborative activity among competitors: per se and rule of reason.[226] The per se analysis is applied to collaborations that have been found to be always or almost always in violation of the antitrust laws because they result in raising prices or reducing output without any appreciable benefit to competition.[227] Only the most egregious collaborations, such as those to fix prices, rig bids, or reduce output, are considered to

---

[220] *See, e.g.*, Aaron J. Burstein, *Amending the ECPA to Enable a Culture of Cybersecurity Research*, 22 HARV. J.L. & TECH. 167 (2008).

[221] 18 U.S.C. §2511(2)(a)(i).

[222] 15 U.S.C. §§1, 4, 15, 26.

[223] 15 U.S.C. §1.

[224] Standard Oil Co. of N.J. v. U.S., 221 U.S. 1, 60 (1911) (interpreting the language of Section One to require that in order for restraints in trade to be considered unlawful, the methods used to restrain the market must be undue or unreasonable).

[225] See Fed. Trade Comm'n & U.S. Dep't of Justice, Antitrust Guidelines for Collaborations Among Competitors (2000), available at http://www ftc.gov/os/2000/04/ftcdojguidelines.pdf (hereinafter Competitor Collaboration Guidelines).

[226] Nat'l Soc'y of Prof'l Eng'rs v. United States, 435 U.S. 679, 692 (1978).

[227] Business Electronics Corp. v. Sharp Electronics Corp., 485 U.S. 717, 723 (1988).

---

be per se illegal.[228] All other collaborations among competitors are subject to review under the rule of reason standard.[229] The rule of reason consists of a flexible inquiry into the potential competitive benefits of an agreement as they are weighed against the potential competitive harms. Most agreements to share information will likely be reviewed under the rule of reason standard.[230] Most collaborations among competitors that exist for the sole purpose of combating cybersecurity threats would be analyzed under the rule of reason standard.

Collaboration among competitors may include a wide variety of activity including research and development, shared manufacturing facilities, and other joint ventures.[231] Agreements to share information may be a part of other broader collaborative activities, or an end unto themselves. The Department of Justice (DOJ), and the Federal Trade Commission (FTC) recognize that information sharing among competitors often has pro-competitive and efficiency-enhancing benefits that may outweigh any anticompetitive risks.[232] The DOJ and the FTC, therefore, have devised guidelines to aid companies in developing collaborative business plans that minimize antitrust concerns.[233] The first aspect of the agreement that the agencies will examine is the extent of the collaboration and the purpose for the collaboration.[234] To the extent that the sharing of information is limited to the purpose of aiding in combating cybersecurity threats, it is likely that the antitrust concerns raised by any potential agreement would be limited as well.[235]

Groups of competitors wishing to collaborate to combat cybersecurity threats, even when following the DOJ and FTC's guidelines, may nonetheless be concerned about antitrust scrutiny. To aid these groups, the DOJ has developed a process for the groups to submit their plans to collaborate to the DOJ for a determination by the agency of whether the proposed collaboration would raise antitrust concerns.[236] It is called the Business Review Procedure. The procedure has been used in the cybersecurity context in the past. For example, the Electric Power Research Institute (EPRI) requested that the DOJ review its proposal to share information related to cyber threats. After examining the proposal, the DOJ issued a business review letter stating that the DOJ was not inclined to initiate an antitrust enforcement action against the collaborative efforts of EPRI on the theory that the proposal would reduce cybersecurity costs and may have a pro-competitive effect.[237] Nonetheless, the DOJ, as it always does in these circumstances, reserved the right to pursue any antitrust concerns should the collaborative effort prove to have a future anticompetitive effect.

---

[228] Competitor Collaboration Guidelines, *supra* note 208, at 3.

[229] *Id.*

[230] Continental T.V. Corp. v. GTE Sylvania Corp., 433 U.S. 36, 49 (1977).

[231] Competitor Collaboration Guidelines, *supra* note 208, at 6-7.

[232] *Id.* at 1.

[233] *Id.*

[234] *Id.* at 12.

[235] See Letter from Joel I. Klein, Assistant Attorney General, Department of Justice, Antitrust Division, to Barbara Greenspan, Associate General Counsel, Electric Power Research Institute, Inc. (October 2, 2000) available at http://justice.gov/atr/public/busreview/6614 htm.

[236] 28 C.F.R. §50.6.

[237] Letter from Joel I. Klein, Assistant Attorney General, Department of Justice, Antitrust Division, to Barbara Greenspan, Associate General Counsel, Electric Power Research Institute, Inc. (October 2, 2000) available at http://justice.gov/atr/public/busreview/6614 htm.

Liability for Information Sharing

Some have argued that sharing or receiving information about cybersecurity threats could potentially expose private sector entities to increased liability. To the extent that ECPA, antitrust laws, or other federal or state laws prohibit private sector entities from sharing cybersecurity threat information amongst themselves or with the government, violating these laws could lead to civil or criminal penalties imposed by the government.[238] Additionally, both ECPA and the antitrust laws provide private rights of action for harmed parties to recover damages from entities that have violated these statutes.[239] Consequently, violating ECPA or the antitrust laws may also expose entities to private civil liability.

Concerns about private civil liability for information sharing may also arise based on the effect that information sharing may have on private civil actions based on injuries caused by a defendant's negligent actions. One way of proving negligence is by convincing a jury that the defendant did not act reasonably in the face of a foreseeable risk.[240] In the absence of a foreseeable risk, a defendant typically has no judicially enforceable duty to mitigate that risk.[241] However, if a defendant has received information about an active cybersecurity threat, then that would tend to show that the risk of attack from such threat was a foreseeable one. In other words, notice of cybersecurity risks might lead a jury to find that the defendant had a duty to act reasonably. For example, if a defendant is using software package X in its information infrastructure, and the defendant receives information from other private sector entities or the government that software package X has been vulnerable to cyberattacks, the receipt of this information may lead a jury to conclude that the defendant was aware of the risk presented by using that software package. If such a duty were found, then the defendant could be liable for any harm that resulted from its negligence.

Receiving information about cybersecurity threats may also be relevant to whether the actions taken by a defendant in the face of a foreseeable risk were reasonable. In order to determine whether a defendant's actions were reasonable, juries are often asked to balance the foreseeable risks of the defendant's actions with the foreseeable risks of the defendant's inaction.[242] For example, shared cybersecurity threat information may include effective and low-cost measures that could be taken to mitigate or prevent a threat. A jury evaluating whether a defendant had acted negligently may find the fact that the defendant had knowledge of effective and low-cost preventative measures may determine that the defendant should be held to a higher standard of care than if the defendant had not received such information.[243]

---

[238] 15 U.S.C. §§1, 4; 18 U.S.C. §§2511, 2701, 3121.

[239] 15 U.S.C. §§15, 26; 18 U.S.C. §§2520, 2707.

[240] *See, e.g.*, First Electric Cooperative Corp. v. Pinson, 642 S.W.2d 301, 303 (Ark. 1982) ("there is no negligence in not guarding against a danger which there is no reason to anticipate").

[241] *Id.*

[242] *E.g.*, Schuldies v. Service Machine Co., 448 F. Supp. 1196, 1199 (E.D. Wis. 1978) ("a person fails to exercise ordinary care when, without intending to do any wrong, he does an act or omits a precaution under circumstances in which a person of ordinary intelligence and prudence ought reasonably to foresee that such act or omission will subject the interests of another to an unreasonable risk of harm").

[243] *E.g.*, Rodriguez v. New Haven, 439 A.2d 421, 424 (Conn. 1981) ("knowledge of a dangerous condition generally requires greater care to meet the standard of reasonable care").

Protection of Proprietary or Confidential Business Information[244]

Sharing cybersecurity threat information may raise concerns about how that information would be used. For example, there may be concerns that other businesses could use the information to gain a competitive advantage. There may also be concerns that cybersecurity threat information shared with the government might be used for regulatory purposes unrelated to cybersecurity. As a result, some private sector entities may be hesitant to voluntarily share cybersecurity-related information with other businesses or with the government.

For example, voluntary sharing of cybersecurity threat information with the government may be inhibited by concerns that such information might be made publicly available under the Freedom of Information Act of 1974 (FOIA), which regulates the disclosure of agency records held by the federal government.[245] Other potential obstacles to sharing information with the government are agency rules or judicial doctrine regarding ex parte communications, the rules of discovery in civil litigation, and state open records laws requiring public disclosure.

Information that is designated as critical infrastructure information (CII) under the Critical Infrastructure Information Act (CIIA) is protected from disclosure under FOIA. Similarly, the CIIA provides that CII will not be subject to agency rules or judicial doctrine regarding ex parte communications. With respect to concerns about litigation, CIIA limits the use of CII in civil litigation and provides that sharing CII with the agency does not count as the "waiver of any applicable privilege or protection provided under law," such as trade secret protection or the attorney-client privilege.[246] CIIA also authorizes the use or disclosure of such information by officers and employees in furtherance of the investigation or the prosecution of a criminal act; or for disclosure to Congress or the Government Accountability Office.

Many of these concerns are also raised in the context of protecting information collected from critical infrastructure, and are discussed in more detail *supra* at "Freedom of Information."

Privacy and Civil Liberties

Privacy and civil liberties advocates argue that several of the proposed cybersecurity information sharing measures go too far in eroding privacy protections.[247] For instance, CISPA and the SECURE IT Act permit private sector use of cybersecurity systems and sharing of cyber threat information "[n]otwithstanding any other provision of law."[248] This provision has the effect of overriding privacy protections such as ECPA and the Privacy Act of 1974. One commentator noted that although some changes are necessary to authorize cyber activities, a broad exclusion of

---

[244] *See* CRS Report R41406, *The Freedom of Information Act and Nondisclosure Provisions in Other Federal Laws* , by Gina Stevens and CRS Report RL33670, *Protection of Security-Related Information*, by Gina Stevens and Todd B. Tatelman.

[245] 5 U.S.C. §552.

[246] *See* Fed. R. Evid. 501.

[247] *See e.g.*, Center for Democracy & Technology, Concerns Mount Over Unresolved Privacy Issues in CISPA, https://www.cdt.org/blogs/greg-nojeim/1804concerns-mount-over-unresolved-privacy-issues-cispa.

[248] H.R. 3523, §2; H.R. 4263, §102(1).

these laws in the cybersecurity area would be "inconsistent with the promise of privacy that undergirds the Wiretap Act and the SCA."[249]

There is also concern among privacy and civil liberties groups that defense agencies like the National Security Agency (NSA) would have access to Internet information obtained through cybersecurity information sharing programs. Generally, defense agencies are not employed in the domestic law enforcement arena.[250] These groups warn that defense agencies like the NSA are not subject to the same oversight and transparency as civilian agencies such as DHS.[251] Observers point to its warrantless wiretapping program in 2001 as proof that the NSA should not be given control over monitoring of domestic Internet activity.[252] These advocates suggest that any proposed information sharing plan clearly state which civilian agencies will have access to this information.[253] This would prevent, in their view, the NSA or other military agencies from inadvertently getting access to this data.

Legislation in the 112th Congress

This section provides a brief description of proposed cybersecurity legislation in the 112th Congress that include regulatory provisions addressing the sharing of cybersecurity threat information amongst the private sector and between the government and the private sector. Particular emphasis has been placed on the provisions that implicate the legal issues discussed above.

H.R. 3523, Cyber Intelligence Sharing and Protection Act of 2011, As Reported

H.R. 3523, the Cyber Intelligence Sharing and Protection Act of 2011 (CISPA), was introduced on November 30, 2011, by Representative Rogers of Michigan, to facilitate sharing of cyber threat intelligence information between the Intelligence Community (IC)[254] and the private sector. On December 1, 2011, the House Permanent Select Committee on Intelligence (HPSCI) held a

---

[249] *Cybersecurity Information Sharing and the Freedom of Information Act: Hearing Before the S. Comm. on the* Judiciary, 112th Cong. (2012) (statement of Paul Rosenzweig, Visiting Fellow, The Heritage Foundation), *available at* http://www.judiciary.senate.gov/pdf/12-3-13RosenzweigTestimony.pdf.

[250] Under the Posse Comitatus Act, the military is prohibited from executing domestic laws. 18 U.S.C. §1385.

[251] Michelle Richardson, *Cybersecurity Information Sharing Legislation and Privacy Implications in the 112th Congress,* AMERICAN CIVIL LIBERTIES UNION (April 16, 2012), http://www.aclu.org/files/assets/ aclu_interested_persons_memo__re__cyber_leg_info_sharing_april_16_2012.pdf.

[252] Greg Nojeim, *Cybersecurity's 7-Step Plan for Internet Freedom*, CENTER FOR DEMOCRACY AND TECHNOLOGY (March 28, 2012), https://www.cdt.org/blogs/greg-nojeim/2803cybersecuritys-8-step-plan-internet-freedom.

[253] *Id.*

[254] Under 50 U.S.C. §401a(4), the IC is comprised of the following offices: the Office of the Director of National Intelligence; the Central Intelligence Agency; the National Security Agency; the Defense Intelligence Agency; the National Geospatial-Intelligence Agency; the National Reconnaissance Office; other offices within the Department of Defense for the collection of specialized national intelligence through reconnaissance programs; the intelligence elements of the Army, the Navy, the Air Force, the Marine Corps, the Coast Guard, the Federal Bureau of Investigation, the Drug Enforcement Administration, and the Department of Energy; the Bureau of Intelligence and Research of the Department of State; the Office of Intelligence and Analysis of the Department of the Treasury; the Office of Intelligence and Analysis of the Department of Homeland Security; and such other elements as may be designated by the President, or designated jointly by the Director of National Intelligence and the head of the department or agency concerned, as an element of the intelligence community.

---

mark up of the bill and favorably ordered reported an amended version to the House.[255] On April 16, 2012, the HPSCI released a discussion draft with new proposed amendments that would be considered when the bill goes to the floor.[256] On April 17, H.R. 3523 was reported with an amendment.[257] The HPSCI released "H.R. 3523–Draft Amendment in the Nature of a Substitute provided to the House Rules Committee–April 19, 2012.[258]

As reported out of the Rules Committee, CISPA would direct the Director of National Intelligence (DNI) to establish procedures under which IC elements would be allowed to share cyber threat intelligence with the private sector and utilities and to encourage sharing.[259] CISPA defines "cyber threat information" as "information directly pertaining to a vulnerability of, or threat to a system or network of a government or private entity, including ... (A) efforts to degrade, disrupt or destroy such system or network; or (B) efforts to gain unauthorized access to a system or network...."[260] Classified cyber threat intelligence information from the IC would only be shareable with entities or persons with appropriate security clearances, and only if sharing would be consistent with the need to protect national security.[261] Entities receiving shared cyber threat intelligence from the IC would be required to take measures to protect that information from unauthorized disclosure.[262] CISPA also directs the DNI to issue guidelines allowing heads of IC elements to grant clearances through an expedited process to employees or officers of certified entities and to certified entities.[263] CISPA explicitly provides that it does not create any right or benefit to cyber threat information as a result of the government's sharing of such information with any public sector entity or utility.

To respond to criticisms about the potential for redisclosure of cyber threat information by recipients, CISPA provides that an entity that receives cyber threat intelligence would be prohibited from further disclosure of such information to an entity other than the federal government or a certified entity, notwithstanding any other provision of law.

In order to address the perceived legal obstacles to information sharing among the private sector, CISPA would give private sector entities the explicit authority to use cybersecurity systems to identify and obtain cybersecurity threat information to protect their rights and property, and to share such information with any other entity, including with the federal government, "notwithstanding any provision of law."[264] Entities that provide cybersecurity goods and services, also known as cybersecurity providers, would have similar authority with the consent of their

---

[255] H. Permanent Select Comm. on Intelligence, Bipartisan Cybersecurity Bill Clears Key Hurdle, December 1, 2011, available at http://intelligence house.gov/press-release/bipartisan-cybersecurity-bill-clears-key-hurdle. See also Lauren Gardner, House Panel Backs Cybersecurity Bill with Stronger Privacy Provisions, CQ, December 1, 2011, available at http://www.cq.com/news.do.

[256] H.R. 3523 (April 16, 2012 - Discussion Draft), *available at* http://intelligence house.gov/sites/ intelligence.house.gov/files/documents/04162012HR3523.pdf.

[257] U.S. Congress, House Permanent Select Committee on Intelligence, The Cyber Intelligence Sharing and Protection Act, report to accompany H.R. 3523, 112th Cong., 2nd sess., 2012, H.Rept. 112-445.

[258] Http://www.rules house.gov/Media/file/PDF_112_2/LegislativeText/CPRT-112-HPRT-RU00-HR3523.pdf.

[259] H.R. 3523, §2 (new §1104(a)(1) of the National Security Act of 1947 (NSA)).

[260] *Id.* (new NSA §1104(b)(f)(6)).

[261] *Id.* (new NSA §1104(a)(2)).

[262] *Id.* (new NSA §1104(a)(2)(C)).

[263] *Id.* (new NSA §1104(a)(3)).

[264] *Id.* (new NSA §§1104(b)(1), (2)).

---

customer to use cybersecurity systems to identify, obtain, and share cyber threat information from the networks of consenting customers, with any other entity designated by the customer including the federal government if designated.[265] The "notwithstanding any provision of law" language means that information sharing is authorized even if another federal or state privacy law, or other law, would protect the information against disclosure.[266] CISPA requires any federal agency or department in receipt of cyber threat information to provide that information to the DHS which is authorized upon request to share such information with another federal agency or department.

The bill would require cyber threat information to be shared subject to restrictions imposed by the submitting entity, including appropriate anonymization or minimization of such information.[267] CISPA would also explicitly prohibit shared information from being used by businesses to gain an unfair competitive advantage to the detriment of the entity sharing the information.[268] CISPA also explicitly exempts information shared with the federal government from disclosure under FOIA and under state or local public disclosure laws.[269] Additionally, the bill would provide that information shared with the federal government be considered proprietary information that could not be disclosed to an entity outside of the federal government, except with the authorization of the entity sharing the information, and could not be used by the government for regulatory purposes.[270] In addition, such information may not be shared by the federal government if it would undermine the purpose for which it was shared; or the federal government recipient determines, unless directed otherwise by the President, that providing the information would undermine the purpose of sharing. The bill also provides that information shared with the federal government be handled consistent with the protection of sources and methods and with national security.

With respect to concerns about increased liability resulting from sharing cybersecurity threat information, CISPA would provide civil and criminal immunity for entities that, acting in good faith, use cybersecurity systems, share information, or make decisions based on such information in accordance with the new authorities created by the bill.[271]

The federal government would be permitted to use shared information for any lawful non-regulatory purpose, provided that at least one significant purpose of the use is a cybersecurity

---

[265] *Id.*

[266] "Congress sometimes seeks to underscore the primacy of a statutory directive by stating that it is to apply "notwithstanding" the provisions of another, specified statute or class of statutes. Courts take into account this expressed intent to override the provisions specified in a "notwithstanding" clause,... but when the clause purports to override "any other provision of law," its preclusive scope often is unclear....As a rule, though, it might be more effective to spell out which other laws are to be disregarded,... and it must be kept in mind, of course, that no "notwithstanding" clause can foreclose subsequent legislation that supersedes it expressly or implicitly." [citations omitted]. CRS Report 97-589, Statutory Interpretation: General Principles and Recent Trends, by Larry M. Eig.

[267] H.R. 3523, (new NSA §1104(b)(2)(A)). Minimization typically refers to limitations on what information is acquired; how it is acquired; how it is maintained; who has access to it within the capturing agency and under what circumstances; to whom and under what circumstances it is disclosed beyond the capturing agency; how long it is preserved; and when and under what circumstances it is expunged. For a discussion of minimization procedures in the context of national security letters, *see* CRS Report R41619, *National Security Letters: Proposals in the 112th Congress*, by Charles Doyle.

[268] *Id.* (new NSA §1104(b)(2)(B)).

[269] *Id.* (new NSA §1104(b)(2)(C)).

[270] *Id.* (new NSA §1104(b)(2)(C)(ii)).

[271] *Id.* (new NSA §1104(b)(3)(A)).

---

purpose or protection of national security.[272] The federal government is also specifically prohibited from searching shared cyber threat information unless it is for the purpose of cybersecurity or protection of national security.[273]

CISPA includes an anti-tasking restriction that explicitly prohibits the government from conditioning the sharing of cyber threat intelligence on the sharing of private sector information with the government.[274]

For the government's intentional or willful violations of the provisions concerning the disclosure, use, or protection of voluntarily shared cyber threat information, CISPA would provide liability for actual damages or $1,000, whichever is greater, plus reasonable attorney fees, and costs.

With respect to concerns about transparency and oversight, CISPA would require an annual unclassified report (with classified annex) by the Intelligence Community Inspector General on the type and use of information shared with the federal government, including actions taken and impacts on privacy and civil liberties.

CISPA would preempt any state or local law that restricts or regulates the use of cybersecurity systems and the sharing of cyber threat information. CISPA would not affect any other authorities for use of a cybersecurity system or to identify, share, or obtain cyber threat intelligence. CISPA does not alter DOD, NSA, or the intelligence communities authority to direct private sector or government cybersecurity efforts. In addition, CISPA does not change existing information sharing relationships, prohibit or require new ones, or modify the government's authority to protect sources and methods and national security.

The Director of National Intelligence must establish and issue procedures and guidelines, in consultation with the Secretary of Homeland Security, to ensure that such procedures and such guidelines permit the owners and operators of critical infrastructure to receive all appropriate cyber threat intelligence in the possession of the federal government; and expeditiously distribute such procedures and such guidelines to departments and agencies of the federal government, private-sector entities, and utilities

H.R. 3674, PRECISE Act

H.R. 3674, the Promoting and Enhancing Cybersecurity and Information Sharing Effectiveness Act of 2011 (PRECISE Act), was introduced on December 15, 2011, by Representative Lungren. On February 1, 2012, the Subcommittee on Cybersecurity, Infrastructure Protection, and Security Technologies of the House Homeland Security Committee held a mark up of the bill, and it was forwarded to the full committee by voice vote. On April 18, 2012, full committee consideration and mark up was held on a substitute bill that changed the information sharing and other provisions. The measure was reported favorably to the full House (as amended) 16-13.[275]

---

[272] *Id.* (new NSA §1104(c)(1)).

[273] *Id.* (new NSA §1104(c)(2)).

[274] *Id.* (new NSA §1104(c)(3)).

[275] H.R. 3674, *available at* http://homeland.house.gov/markup/markup-hr-3674-promoting-and-enhancing-cybersecurity-and-information-sharing-effectiveness.

Section 3 of the PRECISE Act, as reported, would require the Department of Homeland Security to make cyber threat information and other information in DHS's possession available to critical infrastructure owners and operators in a manner that is consistent with statutory and other restrictions on the dissemination of such information.

In addition, section 3 would establish in DHS a National Cybersecurity and Communications Integration Center (NCCIC) for sharing cyber threat information and exchanging technical advice, and assistance. The majority of the members of the advisory board for NCCIC will be from critical infrastructure sectors. NCCIC's charter will be developed by DHS. The NCCIC Board will submit a report to Congress annually on NCCIC's information sharing activities. The DHS is authorized to issue warnings on cybersecurity threats. The DHS may not disclose information that is the basis of the warning without the express consent of the entity that submitted the information. In addition, DHS may not disclose information that is proprietary, business sensitive, relates to the submitting entity, or is not appropriate for public disclosure; and any information restricted by statute, rule, or regulation, and information relating to sources and methods and national security.

S. 2102, Cybersecurity Information Sharing Act of 2012

S. 2102, the Cybersecurity Information Sharing Act of 2012 (CISA), was introduced on February 13, 2012, by Senator Feinstein, for the purpose of improving the sharing of cybersecurity information among entities in the private sector, and between the private sector and the government. The provisions of CISA have also been incorporated, largely without change, into Title VII of S. 2105, the Cybersecurity Act of 2012, as introduced on February 14, 2012.

CISA would address the perceived obstacles to information sharing in existing law by giving private entities affirmative authority to monitor their own information systems for cybersecurity threats, or the information systems of a consenting third party.[276] CISA would also provide explicit authority for private entities to disclose and receive lawfully obtained cybersecurity information so long as the shared information is used for cybersecurity protection and reasonable efforts are made to safeguard individually identifiable information.[277] However, nothing in CISA would be permitted to be construed to authorize price fixing or market allocation between competitors.[278]

Under CISA, the Secretary of DHS would be authorized to designate cybersecurity exchanges, for the purpose of efficiently receiving and distributing cybersecurity threat indicators.[279] Nonfederal entities are explicitly given the authority to provide cybersecurity threat indicators to a cybersecurity exchange, which may only use, retain, or further disclose shared information for the purpose of protecting against or mitigating cybersecurity threats.[280]

---

[276] S. 2102, §2; S. 2105, §701.

[277] S. 2102, §3; S. 2105, §702.

[278] S. 2102, §8(a)(5); S. 2105, §707(a)(5).

[279] S. 2102, §4; S. 2105, §703. The Secretary of DHS would also be required to designate a lead cybersecurity exchange to serve as the focal point within the federal government for cybersecurity information sharing. S. 2102, §4(c); S. 2105, §703(c).

[280] S. 2102, §5; S. 2105, §704. Classified threat information may only be shared with certified entities with adequate security clearances. Security clearances may be granted to certified entities and employees of certified entities. S. 2102, §6; S. 2105, §705.

CISA would provide that information shared with a cybersecurity exchange would be exempt from disclosure under FOIA, as well as any restrictions on *ex parte* communications.[281] Sharing information with a cybersecurity exchange would not constitute a waiver of any applicable privilege regarding the information, including any trade secret protection.[282] Furthermore, no federal entity would be permitted to use a cybersecurity threat indicator as evidence for a regulatory enforcement action against the entity that shared the information.[283]

Federal entities would not be permitted to disclose cybersecurity threat information unless the disclosure is made to protect a federal entity from a cybersecurity threat, or to mitigate a cybersecurity threat to another component, officer, employee, or agent of the federal entity with cybersecurity responsibilities, any cybersecurity exchange, or a private entity that provides a federal entity with an electronic communication service, remote computing service, or cybersecurity service.[284] The recipient of information from a federal entity must also comply with any requirements regarding the protection and further disclosure of such information.[285]

Additional restrictions would apply if cybersecurity threat information was to be shared with law enforcement. Federal cybersecurity exchanges could only disclose information to law enforcement if the information appears to relate to a crime which has been, is being, or is about to be committed, and if minimization procedures developed by the Secretary and approved by the Attorney General permit such disclosure.[286] Federal entities that are not cybersecurity exchanges may use cyber threat information to protect against cybersecurity threats, but must comply with similar restrictions on disclosing shared information to law enforcement.[287] Any disclosure of cyber threat information to a nonfederal entity shall be accompanied by a written agreement under which the recipient of the information agrees that the information will only be used in a manner consistent with the restrictions on disclosures to law enforcement.[288] CISA directs the Secretary of DHS to devise minimization procedures to protect individually identifiable information from unnecessary disclosure.[289] These procedures are to be developed in consultation with privacy and civil liberties experts, the Director of National Intelligence, and the Secretary of Defense.

CISA provides immunity from civil and criminal liability arising from monitoring activities or voluntary disclosure of cyber threat information in compliance with CISA. However, this immunity only applies if the disclosure is made (1) to a cybersecurity exchange, (2) by a provider of cybersecurity services to a customer, (3) to a private entity or governmental entity that provides or manages critical infrastructure, or (4) to any other private entity if the threat information is also provided to a cybersecurity exchange within a reasonable amount of time.[290] Immunity would also be provided if an entity acts in good faith reliance that such actions are

---

[281] S. 2102, §§5(d), (e); S. 2105, §§704(d), (e).

[282] S. 2102, §5(f); S. 2105, §704(f).

[283] S. 2102, §7(c); S. 2105, §706(c).

[284] S. 2102, §5(g)(1)(A); S. 2105, §704(g)(1)(A).

[285] S. 2102, §5(g)(1)(B); S. 2105, §704(g)(1)(B).

[286] S. 2102, §5(g)(2); S. 2105, §704(g)(2).

[287] S. 2102, §5(g)(3); S. 2105, §704(g)(3).

[288] S. 2102, §5(g)(3)(B); S. 2105, §704(g)(3)(B).

[289] S. 2102, §5(g)(4); S. 2105, §704(g)(4).

[290] S. 2102, §7(a); S. 2105, §706(a).

permitted by CISA.[291] No liability protections would attach to conduct that knowingly and willfully violates CISA.[292] With respect to negligence based actions, CISA would bar civil or criminal liability based on the reasonable failure to act on information received. No breach of contract claims could be brought based on compliance with lawful restrictions placed on shared information.[293] However, none of these protections could be construed to limit liability for a failure to comply with the requirements imposed on the use and protection of information.[294]

S. 2105, Cybersecurity Act of 2012

Title VII of the S. 2105, the Cybersecurity Act of 2012, contains virtually the same provisions as S. 2102, the Cybersecurity Information Sharing Act of 2012, discussed above. While Title VII of S. 2105 authorizes the Secretary of Homeland Security to designate both federal and nonfederal entities as cybersecurity exchanges, with the goal of "efficiently receiv[ing] and distribut[ing] cybersecurity threat indicators...."[295] Title III of the bill would also address this need by directing the new National Center for Cybersecurity and Communications (NCCC or Center) to create its own information sharing program.[296] Specifically, the NCCC would be charged with creating an information sharing system that collects information from and redistributes information to federal agencies, state and local governments, national information infrastructure, critical infrastructure, and the private sector. Both federal agencies and critical infrastructure would have an affirmative obligation to provide certain information to the Center's information sharing program.[297] Other entities, including state and local governments and private sector actors, would be permitted to participate voluntarily in the program.[298]

It may not be clear how these separate authorities would interact. For example, under Title VII, DHS would be required to designate a lead cybersecurity exchange within 60 days of the enactment of the act.[299] Following this interim period, which can only last 60 days, it is unclear if the NCCC program will be designated as a cybersecurity exchange. If the NCCC program is designated as an exchange, either the lead or an additional federal exchange,[300] the restrictions and protections outlined in Title VII would likely apply. Title VII creates specific limitations on the use of information in the exchange by federal entities,[301] nonfederal entities,[302] and the exchange itself.[303] Additionally, information shared in an exchange is explicitly exempted from Freedom of Information Act requests[304] and ex parte communications limitations.[305] Title VII also

---

[291] S. 2102, §7(b); S. 2105, §706(b).

[292] S. 2102, §7(f); S. 2105, §706(f).

[293] S. 2102, §7(e); S. 2105, §706(e).

[294] S. 2102, §7(g); S. 2105, §706(g).

[295] S. 2105 §703(a)-(b).

[296] S. 2105 §301 (new HSA §243).

[297] S. 2105 §301 (new HSA §243(b)(1)(B), (c)(1)(B)).

[298] S. 2105 §301 (new HSA §243(c)(1)(C)).

[299] S. 2105 §703(c)(3)(A). Until this designation is finalized, the National Cybersecurity and Communications Integration Center (NCCIC) would serve as the interim lead exchange. S. 2105 §703(c)(3)(B).

[300] S. 2105 §703(d).

[301] S. 2105 §704(g).

[302] S. 2105 §704(c).

[303] S. 2105 §704(b), (g).

[304] *See* 5 U.S.C. §552.

provides immunity from liability based on lawfully obtained cybersecurity information that is voluntarily disclosed to an exchange.[306] Finally, exchanges are bound by specific requirements regarding with whom an exchange can share classified information, including restricting access to people with "an appropriate security clearance."[307]

However, if the NCCC program is not designated as an exchange, it arguably appears that Title VII would not apply to the program at all. Title III includes far fewer restrictions on the use of the information gathered by the Center's program. Notably, Title III provides the Center much greater discretion in disseminating classified information, only instructing the Director to create procedures to ensure classified information is "appropriately shared between and among appropriate Federal and non-Federal entities...."[308] However, unlike Title VII exchanges, Title III does not specifically restrict who can receive classified information from the NCCC information sharing program. Furthermore, Title III does not provide protection from liability for entities that provide information to the NCCC program, even though certain entities, like covered critical infrastructure, are required to disclose incident-related information.[309]

S. 2151, SECURE IT Act

S. 2151, the Strengthening and Enhancing Cybersecurity by Using Research, Education, Information, and Technology Act of 2012 (SECURE IT Act), was introduced by Senator McCain on March 1, 2012. Title I of the SECURE IT Act addresses the sharing of cybersecurity threat information among the private sector and between the private sector and the public sector.

Notwithstanding any other provision of law, the SECURE IT Act would give private sector entities the explicit authority to employ countermeasures and use cybersecurity systems to identify, obtain, or otherwise possess cyber threat information for the purpose of preventing, investigating, or otherwise mitigating threats to information security.[310] This authority applies to networks owned by an entity, or to other networks as authorized by the other networks' owner.[311] Entities would also be authorized to disclose cyber threat information to a cybersecurity center[312] or to any other entity for the same purposes.[313] Entities that provide information security products or services, also known as information security providers, would also be permitted to obtain, identify, possess, or disclose cyber threat information encountered in the course of providing such

---

(...continued)

[305] S. 2105 §704(d)(1), (e).

[306] S. 2105 §706(a)(2).

[307] S. 2105 §705(a).

[308] S. 2105 §301 (new HSA §243(a)(2)).

[309] *See* S. 2105 §301 (new HSA §243(c)(1)(B).

[310] S. 2151, §102(a)(1).

[311] *Id.*

[312] The bill defines the term cybersecurity center to mean the Department of Defense Cyber Crime Center, the Intelligence Community Incident Response Center, the United States Cyber Command Joint Operations Center, the National Cyber Investigative Joint Task Force, the National Security Agency/Central Security Service Threat Operations Center, the National Cybersecurity and Communications Integration Center, and any successor center. S. 2151, §101(5).

[313] S. 2151, §102(a)(2).

---

services. However, customers must be given a reasonable opportunity to authorize or prevent any disclosure, or to request anonymization of such information.[314]

Private entities would be permitted to share information directly with each other, but recipients of cybersecurity threat information would be obligated to comply with restrictions (such as anonymization) set forth by the entity providing the information.[315] Shared information may not be used to obtain an unfair competitive advantage. The act of sharing would not be considered a violation of the antitrust laws if shared to assist with information security.[316]

Providers of electronic communication services, remote computing services, or cybersecurity services to a federal agency or department would be required to provide any cyber threat information related to the provision of such services that is in the provider's possession.[317] The provider is also permitted to provide this threat information to a cybersecurity center,[318] and the notified federal department or agency is required to provide the threat information with a cybersecurity center.[319] A cybersecurity center would be required to share information with other cybersecurity centers,[320] and may disclose such information to other federal entities for cybersecurity or national security purposes, or for the prevention, investigation, or prosecution of any of the crimes that are eligible for an interception order under ECPA.[321] Such information may also be disclosed to a provider of electronic communication services, remote computing services, or cybersecurity services, for purposes related to those services.[322]

The SECURE IT Act would place restrictions on how information shared with cybersecurity centers could be disclosed or used.[323] Except for the disclosures provided in the preceding paragraph, information shared with a cybersecurity center could not be disclosed by the cybersecurity center without the consent of the entity that provided the information.[324] Information shared with a cybersecurity center would also be exempt from disclosure under FOIA and similar state or local laws requiring disclosure.[325] Shared information would also not be subject to any restrictions on *ex parte* communications.[326] Federal, state, tribal, and local governments would be prohibited from using or disclosing shared information for regulatory purposes.[327]

---

[314] S. 2151, §102(a)(3).

[315] S. 2151, §§102(e)(1), (2).

[316] S. 2151, §102(e)(3).

[317] S. 2151, §102(b)(1).

[318] *Id.*

[319] S. 2151, §102(b)(2).

[320] S. 2151, §102(d)(1)(B).

[321] S. 2151, §102(c)(1)(A).

[322] S. 2151, §102(c)(1)(B).

[323] S. 2151, §102(c).

[324] S. 2151, §102(c)(2) (requiring prior consent for disclosures to state, tribal, and local governments for criminal prevention, investigation, or prosecution); S. 2151, §102(c)(3) (requiring prior consent for disclosures outside of the federal government); S. 2151, §102(c)(7) (requiring prior consent for subsequent disclosures of information shared with state, tribal, and local governments).

[325] S. 2151, §§102(c)(4), (5), (7).

[326] S. 2151, §102(c)(6).

[327] S. 2151, §102(c)(8). However, the procedures to implement the SECURE IT Act would not be considered "regulatory" for the purposes of this limitation. *Id.*

In order to address concerns that private sector entities may have about liability, the SECURE IT Act provides civil and criminal immunity for actions authorized under the bill.[328] Additionally, no cause of action would be permitted against an entity for using, receiving, or disclosing cyber threat information, or for any act or omission following the lawful receipt of such information.[329] Notwithstanding these provisions, no immunity would be provided for unlawful disclosures of classified information.[330]

Preemption

As the body of federal cybersecurity law grows, the possibility that it will preempt conflicting state law will increase with it. After September 11, 2001, states took various measures to protect their critical infrastructure. This included defining "critical infrastructure," creating security standards for these entities, and carving out exceptions under public disclosure laws so vital information would not get into the hands of bad actors.

It is well established that the Supremacy Clause of the United States Constitution can invalidate any state law that interferes with or is contrary to federal law.[331] This is known as preemption. The preemptive effect of a federal statute can be either expressly stated in the statute or implied by the structure and purpose of the legislation.[332] If there is express language, the court will interpret the words used by Congress and assume that the ordinary meaning of the text expresses the legislative purpose.[333] For example, if Congress uses broad language in its preemption provision, the court will construe its preemptive effect broadly.[334] Absent explicit preemptive language, there are two types of implied preemption: (1) field preemption, where the federal regime is "so pervasive to make the reasonable inference that Congress left no room for the States to supplement it";[335] and (2) conflict preemption, where state law "stands as an obstacle to the accomplishment and execution of the full purposes and objectives of Congress."[336]

Because any preemption analysis relies on congressional intent, the language of the statute is of primary importance. Many of the proposals provide explicit language preempting state laws. For example, Title I of S. 2105, the Cybersecurity Act of 2012, contains an express preemption provision, stating: "This Act shall supersede any statute, provision of a statute, regulation, or rule of a State or political subdivision of a State that expressly requires comparable cybersecurity practices to protected covered critical infrastructure."[337] This section is followed by a savings

---

[328] S. 2151, §102(g)(1)(A).

[329] S. 2151, §102(g)(1)(B).

[330] S. 2151, §102(g)(2).

[331] Hillsborough County v. Automated Med. Labs., Inc., 471 U.S. 707, 713 (1985).

[332] Gade v. Nat'l Solid Wastes Mgmt. Ass'n, 505 U.S. 88, 98 (1992).

[333] Morales v. TWA, 504 U.S. 374, 383 (1992).

[334] Metropolitan Life Ins. Co. v. Massachusetts, 471 U.S. 724, 739 (1985).

[335] Fidelity Fed. Sav. & Loan Assn. v. De le Cuesta, 458 U.S. 141, 152-53 (1982) (quoting Rice v. Sante Fe Elevator Corp., 331 U.S. 218, 230 (1947)).

[336] Hines v. Davidowitz, 312 U.S. 52, 67 (1941).

[337] S. 2105, §111(a).

clause that states: "Except as expressly provided in subsection (a) and section 105(e), nothing in this Act shall be construed to preempt the applicability of any other State law or requirement."[338]

Because the scope of "covered critical infrastructure" has yet to be determined, it is impossible to identify with specificity which state critical infrastructure laws would be preempted by this provision of the Cybersecurity Act of 2012. However, certain categories of state laws may be more likely to be preempted, such as those that directly regulate industrial facilities. For example, New Jersey has enacted the Toxic Catastrophe Prevention Act which was designed to prevent the release of hazardous substances from industrial plants and provide an abatement and evacuation plan in the event a catastrophic release occurs.[339] That act requires that an owner or operator of a covered facility establish a risk management program. Likewise, Maryland requires that any facility where hazardous materials are stored analyze the security of the facility every five years in accordance with rules adopted by the Department of State Police.[340] Similarly, New York requires the commissioner of the state division of homeland security to review security measures for all critical infrastructure relating to energy generation and transmission in the state every five years.[341] The state public service commission has the discretion whether to require the owners of these facilities to implement these plans. The application of these and other similar state requirements to covered critical infrastructure may be preempted if they are "comparable" to the risk-based performance standards to be established by the Secretary of DHS under the Cybersecurity Act of 2012.

It could also be argued that the broad language "comparable security practices," coupled with a savings clause that fails to carve out exceptions for state regulation of covered critical infrastructure, evidences Congress's intent to cover the whole field of protecting critical infrastructures.[342] Further, DHS may argue for a broad construction of this preemption provision as it has argued in the past that "the law of preemption recognizes that state laws must give way to Federal statutes and regulatory programs to ensure a unified and coherent national approach in areas where the Federal interests prevail—such as national security."[343] Because cybersecurity has been equated with national security, this deference theory could apply here.[344]

Cybersecurity legislation to encourage sharing of cybersecurity threat information may also preempt state laws. For example, all fifty states have included electronic communications in their respective wiretap laws which prohibit the interception and disclosure of certain

---

[338] S. 2105, §111(b).

[339] N.J. Stat. Ann. §13:1K-19.

[340] Md. Env. Code §7-701.

[341] N.Y. Exec. Law §713 (2011).

[342] Cf. 15 U.S.C. §7707(b). In the Controlling the Assault of Non-Solicited Pornography and Marketing Act of 2003 (CAN-SPAM), P.L. 108-187, 117 Stat. 2699, Congress included a broad clause preempting all state laws from regulating the use of electronic mail to send commercial messages, but also carved out an exception for any state statute that prohibited "falsity or deception." With no such exception in S. 2105, it may be inferred that Congress intended to preempt the whole field of regulating critical infrastructures.

[343] Chemical Facility Anti-Terrorism Standards, 71 *Federal Register* 78,276, 78,293 (December 28, 2006).

[344] *See* President Barack Obama, Remarks on Securing Our Nation's Cyber Infrastructure (May 29. 2009) ("[I]t's now clear this cyber threat is one of the most serious economic and national security challenges we face as a nation."), available at http://www.whitehouse.gov/the-press-office/remarks-president-securing-our-nations-cyber-infrastructure; *cf.* Michael Jo, *National Security Preemption: The Case of Chemical Safety Regulation*, 85 N.Y.U. L. Rev. 2065, 2087 (2010).

communications.[345] However, S. 2102, the Cybersecurity Information Sharing Act contains an explicit preemption clause with respect to information sharing. Section 8(b) reads:

> This Act supersedes any law or requirement of a State or political subdivision of a State that restricts or otherwise expressly regulates the provision of cybersecurity services or the acquisition, interception, retention, use or disclosure of communications, records, or other information by private entities to the extent such law contains requirements inconsistent with this Act.[346]

The provisions of S. 2102, including this preemption clause, were also incorporated into Title VII of S. 2105. Similarly, H.R. 3523, the Cyber Intelligence Sharing and Protection Act (CISPA), contains a preemption clause providing that the bill would supersede "any statute of a State or political subdivision of a State that restricts or otherwise expressly regulates an activity authorized under subsection (b) [which authorizes private sector entities to use of cybersecurity systems to identify, obtain, or share cyber threat information]."[347] Likewise, H.R. 3674, the PRECISE Act, would "supersede[] any statute of a State or political subdivision of a State that restricts or otherwise expressly regulates the acquisition, interception, retention, use, or disclosure of communications, records, or other information" by private or government entities to the extent that such statute is inconsistent.[348] Similarly, the SECURE IT Act provides that it supersedes any state law that restricts or otherwise expressly regulates an activity authorized by the bill.[349] All of these provisions would likely be read to preempt the body of state wiretapping laws, to the extent that application of those laws would prevent the sharing of cybersecurity information authorized under the proposed legislation.[350] These bills could also preempt state data breach notification laws.[351] These bills could also preempt common law torts such as invasion of privacy or statutory remedies such as California's "Shine the Light" law, which regulates when and how a business can share a customer's personal information.[352]

State open records laws are another category that would likely be preempted under recent cybersecurity legislation being considered by Congress. Currently, states take a varied approach to exempting security information from state FOIA requirements.[353] Some states, including Indiana[354] and Alabama,[355] provide for specific disclosure exemptions for certain categories of information such as vulnerable assets or security plans. Others states, including Maryland, simply

---

[345] NATIONAL CONFERENCE OF STATE LEGISLATURES, ELECTRONIC SURVEILLANCE LAW, http://www.ncsl.org/issues-research/telecom/electronic-surveillance-laws.aspx.

[346] S. 2102, §8(b). The use of "inconsistent" could be construed as "conflict" preemption language, intended only to displace those laws that would impede DHS's ability to create the information sharing programs.

[347] H.R. 3523, §2(a).

[348] *Id.*

[349] S. 2151, §102(f)(1); H..R. 4263, §102(f)(1).

[350] NATIONAL CONFERENCE OF STATE LEGISLATURES, ELECTRONIC SURVEILLANCE LAW, http://www.ncsl.org/issues-research/telecom/electronic-surveillance-laws.aspx. For a list of state wiretap laws, see appendices in CRS Report 98-326, *Privacy: An Overview of Federal Statutes Governing Wiretapping and Electronic Eavesdropping*, by Gina Stevens and Charles Doyle.

[351] See CRS Report R42475, *Data Security Breach Notification Laws*, by Gina Stevens 4, n.21.

[352] CAL. CIV. CODE §1798.83.

[353] *See* National Association of Regulatory Utility Commissioners, Information Sharing Practices in Regulated Critical Infrastructure States (2007), http://www.naruc.org/Publications/NARUC%20CIP%20Information%20FIN.pdf.

[354] IND. CODE §5-14-3-4.

[355] ALA. CODE §36-12-40.

---

provide that anything protected under the federal FOIA statute is protected under their state statute.[356] Still others have more broadly stated FOIA protections such as "in the public interest," as used in Arkansas.[357] However, the PRECISE Act and the SECURE IT Act explicitly provide that cybersecurity information shared with state and local governments shall not be subject to any state or local law requiring disclosure of information or records.[358] Both the Cybersecurity Act of 2012 and CISA similarly provide that information shared with a cybersecurity exchange designated under the bills would be exempt from FOIA "or any comparable State law."[359]

Author Contact Information

Edward C. Liu
Legislative Attorney
eliu@crs.loc.gov, 7-9166

Gina Stevens
Legislative Attorney
gstevens@crs.loc.gov, 7-2581

Kathleen Ann Ruane
Legislative Attorney
kruane@crs.loc.gov, 7-9135

Alissa M. Dolan
Legislative Attorney
adolan@crs.loc.gov, 7-8433

Richard M. Thompson II
Legislative Attorney
rthompson@crs.loc.gov, 7-8449

---

[356] MD. CODE ANN. STATE GOV'T §10-615(2).

[357] ARK. CODE. ANN. §23-2-316.

[358] H.R. 3674, §3; S. 2151, §102(f)(3).

[359] S. 2102, §5(d); S. 2105, §704(d).